Bushcraft
Basics

Bushcraft Basics

A Common Sense Wilderness Survival Handbook

Leon Pantenburg

Skyhorse Publishing

Skyhorse Publishing books may be purchased in bulk at special discounts for sales promotion, corporate gifts, fund-raising, or educational purposes. Special editions can also be created to specifications. For details, contact the Special Sales Department, Skyhorse Publishing, 307 West 36th Street, 11th Floor, New York, NY 10018 or info@skyhorsepublishing.com.

Skyhorse® and Skyhorse Publishing® are registered trademarks of Skyhorse Publishing, Inc.®, a Delaware corporation.

Visit our website at www.skyhorsepublishing.com.

10 9 8 7 6 5 4 3 2 1

Library of Congress Cataloging-in-Publication Data is available on file.

Cover design by Tom Lau
Cover photo credit: Getty Images

Print ISBN: 978-1-5107-5191-0
Ebook ISBN: 978-1-5107-5192-7

Printed in China

DEDICATION

This book is dedicated to my wife, Debbie, who got me started writing in the preparedness and survival field many years ago, and my children Dan, Jimmy, and Mary—all of you are the reason I prepare for whatever emergencies might happen.

I also appreciate the lessons learned with my siblings, Joan, Linda, Karla, Carmen, Elaine, Susan, and Michael—growing up on an Iowa farm taught us the value of self-sufficiency for a lifetime of the unexpected—nobody ever had a more supportive backup group or better friends.

Because of my group of cousins, aunts, and uncles, I had a wonderful childhood. And if I could have picked out my nieces and nephews, I could not have done better. The in-laws added later have immensely enriched my life.

Finally, to the memory of James "Jimmy" Patrick Pantenburg, April 21, 1994 to July 3, 2009, I think about and miss you every day. See ya later!

And thank you, Lord, for the many blessings you continually shower upon me.

TABLE OF CONTENTS

A survival situation can occur during the most typical times of your life. Whether you're riding home from work and disaster strikes, or you take a wrong turn on a remote road, your life will depend on your reaction.

INTRODUCTION
WHY I STARTED SURVIVAL COMMON SENSE

I've been an outdoors enthusiast for as long as I can remember. I'm outside year round, and my favorite season is whichever season it happens to be at the time.

My wildest dreams never included editing a bushcrafting and wilderness survival website.

I've been an outdoor enthusiast for as long as I can remember, and was a Boy Scout leader and Girl Scout volunteer for years as well. In those capacities, I taught or helped to teach bushcrafting, wilderness survival, and various out-door skills. I did this for fun and never thought about how my teaching skills might be important down the road. During this time, I learned a tremendous amount from other skilled instructors.

Before I retired from my day job in November 2017, I was an instructor and mentor for communications students at Central Oregon Community College in Bend, Oregon. I spent most of my career as a journalist, writing feature stories about interesting people and places, and for years I was an investigative reporter.

Indirectly, that background led to writing a survival blog. In 2006, I was working for *The Bulletin* newspaper in Bend. Within a one-month period, two people died of hypothermia after becoming lost in the backcountry. Subsequently, I was given an investigative assignment to write a winter survival guide for Central Oregon.

This research opened my eyes. I couldn't believe the widespread misinformation and just plain "fake news" and articles that were promoted as fact. The result of my assignment was my *Winter Survival Guide* that was published in 2007. It went over very well, and received several awards.

Concurrently, I was helping teach scouts and kids basic wilderness skills. After one session, a parent commented:

"What you teach is so simple and easy. *Survival* is just *common sense.*" At that instant, I knew that was a title or name for something.

Also, I grew increasingly concerned about the proliferation of reality "survival" shows on TV. While the shows do get people interested in the concept of survival, most of these programs sacrifice valid information for higher ratings. Some of the participants' shenanigans are dangerous, and provide a very bad role model for inexperienced viewers.

My wife, Debbie, tired of hearing me rant and rave about dangerous advice, non-realistic programming, and charlatan survival instructors. She lined up an initial website, and essentially said to me, "Put up or shut up." So, I stopped ranting and started writing.

My survival blog, *SurvivalCommonSense.com*, came online in October, 2009, a few months after my middle son died of cancer. It was a grievous period and I buried my head in writing. The website was a way to focus my thoughts and, hopefully, help keep someone else's family from suffering through a tragedy.

Initially, the website was intended only as a resource for scout volunteers, and I figured a small, select group of scout volunteers might occasionally view it. To my continued amazement and appreciation, people from all over the world follow the site, and now *SurvivalCommonSense.com* receives thousands of page views daily and has reached hundreds of thousands of people. The *"Survival Common Sense"* YouTube page has more than 250 videos with more than eight million views.

Here's why it works. I never claim to know everything. But I do know a lot of experts on survival subjects, and my interviewing skills and investigative experience means my "bull alarm" is finely-tuned. I question and test everything.

I truly love learning and teaching wilderness skills, and I hope this book gets you interested too!

CHAPTER 1
WHERE TO BEGIN

"Do the difficult things while they are easy and do the great things while they are small. A journey of a thousand miles must begin with a single step."
–Lao Tzu

Hurricanes. Flooding. Tornadoes. Earthquakes. Forest fires. It doesn't matter where you live. Chances are there are some potential natural disasters that could change your life. And we are seeing this happen more and more all the time.

So how do you prepare for these epochs? *Can* you prepare for them? Most importantly, ask yourself this question:

Can I dunk a basketball?

I can't. Never could. But watch any NBA game and see the guys slam the ball home at every opportunity.

Here's the point: If you watch the survival and bushcraft "reality" shows you may see incredible techniques done routinely, under the worst circumstances. So what? Use your common sense filter.

Just because somebody can dunk a basketball or perform wondrous bushcraft techniques on TV doesn't mean you can, or can learn just by watching others. Don't rely on gee-whiz technology or esoteric aboriginal survival techniques. The idea is to survive during a disaster: *There is no time for on-the-job training!*

Copyright Pantenburg Photography

A natural disaster may disrupt electricity, natural gas and water, and shut down road infrastructure for days. Always prepare to walk home and shelter in place.

You've just started to prepare by reading this far. You have acknowledged that you may need to know more and this book is a good first step. Until you know what event or situation you need to be prepared for, you can't know what you don't know.

There are instances where bushcrafting and survival skills may prove invaluable in rural and even urban and big city disasters.

For example, being able to make a campfire and rig up a tarp shelter are great bushcraft skills to know in the wilderness. But how about in the aftermath of a flood, hurricane, or tornado where you may be isolated because of high water or downed bridges and power lines?

Imagine an earthquake. Your high rise is evacuated, you're out in the parking lot, and nobody can get in or out. You might be stranded in the rain or foul weather, and a campfire and tarp shelter might be just what you need.

So, city dwellers need wilderness survival and bushcraft skills too. And bushcrafting and preparedness go hand-in-hand.

Five Bushcrafting Skills for Urban Survival

Emergency preparedness bags had already been set up for my daughter, wife, and son at our home. Then my daughter started college near Los Angeles in 2014. I beefed up her bag with more food, water containers, extra flashlights, and batteries.

I've always been paranoid about the potential for a major earthquake in the Los Angeles area. Then, in an instant, I went from being a slightly-weird-but-harmless dad to a visionary as a 6.0 earthquake rocked Napa, California.

That was a great segue into a common question:

"What wilderness survival skills will work in an urban emergency situation?"

I believe bushcrafting and wilderness survival skills will work anywhere. Emergency situations—anywhere—have several things in common. These include:

- Survival situations are unexpected and can happen in an instant.
- Everyone's initial response will probably be one of disbelief, something like, "This can't be happening."
- The situation could escalate into one of chaos and confusion.
- The situation may become life-threatening if people react wrong.
- Most people won't have a clue about what to do next.
- Widespread panic is always possible.

Any survival skills training must be accompanied by a survival mindset. You have to make up your mind to prevail, and be able to make a plan that will sustain you through the disaster. So, let's say an earthquake, hurricane, tornado, forest fire (or fill in your particular local disaster) has occurred. You have to evacuate your office building and end up in a parking lot with a lot of other people. The weather is nasty; it's raining and the temperature is dropping. The roads are blocked and there is no help in the immediate, foreseeable future. What skills do you need?

Here are five wilderness survival skills that could help you survive an urban emergency:

1. **Shelter:** Your first consideration might be getting out of the elements. Do you know how to tie effective knots? Can you make a tarp shelter if you have to? Can you improvise some sort of refuge from the elements, using available materials?

   Maybe the best place to find shelter materials is in the nearby dumpster. Look for anything that can insulate you from the elements: plastic sheeting, newspapers, cardboard, etc. Or you might want to take shelter in the dumpster itself.

   Check out trash cans—if it has a 42- or 55-gallon plastic bag liner, you can make a quick shelter out of it. The smaller trash can bags can be useful for a myriad of tasks—keeping tinder dry, as a container for gathering wood, as a head covering in the rain, for gathering rain water for drinking, etc.

2. **Water:** Any water you might find should be suspect, unless it is bottled or otherwise sealed from contamination. A water purification filter or chemical purification materials could be worth their weight in gold. (I have used the Polar Pure chemical purification system extensively, and recommend this product.)

3. **Fire:** You should know how to build a campfire using whatever flammable materials are available. Many of the people in the parking lot might need a place to warm up, and as it gets dark, light will be greatly appreciated. Also, boiling water is usually the quickest way to purify it. Make sure to grab any containers from the dumpster—you may need them later.

   Obviously, if you smell gas or the situation seems dangerous, don't play with fire!

4. **Navigation:** Maybe you have to leave the area because staying would be dangerous. Do you know where to go, and how to get

there? Can you read a city street map and use a compass? During a storm, or in the darkness, you may not be able to determine directions. Know how to read a map, and be able to orient it by using streets and visible landmarks.

5. **First aid:** Everybody should take a basic first-aid class. You don't have to reach EMT or First Responder expertise, but a rudimentary knowledge is important. After any sort of disaster, somebody will be hurt, and you may be the only one available to help. So grab the first-aid kit from the break room on the way out of the building!

Obviously, there are a lot of other skills that you should know or learn. If you practice and prepare for an earthquake, for example, that means you're pretty well set for other disasters. You can't prepare for every eventuality, but you can come close!

Get the appropriate maps for the area and know how to read them. Bridges and other infrastructures could be damaged and you may need to make detours around bottlenecks on the roads.

My friend, Matt Banton, and I took a Wilderness First Aid Class together. Among other skills, we learned how to splint a broken limb.

Recommended Reading

A library of reference books is a great idea, and it may be the first area you need to work on.

Here are my fifteen favorite books that might help you on your bushcrafting and preparedness journey:

1. *Surviving a Wilderness Emergency* by Peter Kummerfeldt

Peter Kummerfeldt has walked the talk in the wilderness survival field for decades. I met him at an outdoor expo about fifteen years ago. Peter was doing a session on outdoor survival myths and I sat in out of curiosity.

This led to a "Born Again" wilderness survival experience. I went to every other session Kummerfeldt did that day, and followed him back to his booth to talk some more. That night, I went home and threw away three items I had been carrying in my backcountry survival gear for years.

Kummerfeldt was born in Kenya, East Africa, then came to America in 1965 and joined the US Air Force. He is a graduate of the Air Force Survival Instructor Training School and has served as an instructor at the Basic Survival School in Spokane, Washington, the Arctic

A library of survival, bushcraft, and preparedness publications should be part of everyone's preparedness equipment.

Survival School in Fairbanks, Alaska, and the Jungle Survival School in the Republic of the Philippines. For twelve years, Kummerfeldt was the Survival Training Director at the United States Air Force Academy in Colorado Springs, Colorado. He retired from the Air Force in 1995 after thirty years of service.

He has addressed over twenty thousand people as the featured speaker at numerous seminars, conferences, and national conventions. He is a featured writer on my website *SurvivalCommonSense.com*.

Surviving a Wilderness Emergency *by Peter Kummerfeldt is one of my go-to bushcrafting and wilderness survival books.*

2. *Build the Perfect Survival Kit* by John D. McCann

I believe everyone should have a survival kit handy at all times. But what if you don't know just what to include in a kit, or how to make one?

This book will solve that quandary. McCann draws on a wealth of experience and skill to help the reader craft a kit that will work for their personal situations and ability levels. This book is on my survival shelf and I frequently refer to it.

3. *The Unthinkable* by Amanda Ripley

Suppose that your significant other isn't into preparedness. What is the first thing you can do to get them thinking about the possibility of the "unthinkable" happening? The answer: hand them a copy of this book.

The Unthinkable is not about disaster recovery. It's about what happens in the midst of one—before emergency personnel arrive and structure is imposed upon the situation. It's about the human reaction to disaster and how you should act if you want to survive.

The book is not about stockpiling food, tools, weapons, or prepping. You must understand what goes on in your head during a disaster before you can use your tools. You'll need information and techniques to respond correctly, which is provided in *The Unthinkable*.

4. *Survival Psychology* by Dr. John Leach

Some thirty years before the rash of "reality" or "survival" shows, came this book about people's reactions to emergency situations based on psychological studies.

Survival Psychology by John Leach, PhD, of the University of Lancaster, England, was a groundbreaking text, which today is a reference source for many bushcraft and survival bestsellers. If some of Leach's writing or thoughts sound familiar, it is because you've read or heard them before!

Leach found that in any emergency, eighty percent of the people present won't have any idea what to do, ten to fifteen percent will do the wrong thing, and only ten to fifteen percent will act appropriately. The small group of people who will survive react based on prior training.

Until you know what might happen in your mind, or in the heads of the people around you, there's no way to come up with a plan to survive.

5. *The Survival Medicine Handbook* by Joseph Alton, MD and Amy Alton, ARNP

Better known as Dr. Bones and Nurse Amy, the duo is widely regarded in the preparedness industry as the go-to couple for all things medical. Their stated goal is: "To put a medically prepared person in every family for any disaster."

First aid manuals are common, and come in all shapes, configurations, and sizes. There is a plethora of information about taking care of injuries on the trail. But most of the ones I've seen, including those designed for Third World areas, always end up recommending that readers seek modern medical help.

That's where this manual is different. What happens if a disaster overwhelms emergency responders? Or if a catastrophe, such as a flood or earthquake, prevents entrance into an area?

6. *Food Storage for Self-Sufficiency and Survival* by Angela Paskett

There are some very good how-to books for food storage. But *Food Storage for Self-Sufficiency and Survival* by Angela Paskett stands out from the rest, and it bears looking into further.

I met Angela Paskett several years ago at a Food Insurance gathering. It was evident that Paskett knew her stuff when it came to storing and preserving food. At the time, Paskett mentioned she was working on a food storage book which has since been published.

Food Storage is not a cookbook (though there are some great recipes in it) or a complete survival manual. It is a nuts-and-bolts guide for storing food.

It is informative, an easy read, and packed with information for newcomers and experienced prepper types. Paskett writes in an engaging, informative style that is very appealing, and you'll find yourself drawn into the subject.

7. Deep Survival: Who Lives, Who Dies, and Why by Lawrence Gonzales

I read *Deep Survival* in a few marathon sessions. The fast-paced accounts of real life survival situations are mesmerizing. It's a good read to get you started on creating your own survival mindset.

This book features useful information for anybody who practices survival common sense, since a survival mindset must be established before you can use any tools and training you might have acquired.

In the book, Gonzales mentions twelve points that disaster survivors seem to have in common. These points are definitely worth contemplation, even if you don't get anything else out of the text.

8. Call of the Mild: Learning to Hunt My Own Dinner by Lily Raff McCaulou

The book traces Lily Raff McCaulou's journey from being a big city dweller with no hunting experience to becoming an enthusiastic hunter. It is the story of her personal evolution.

Reared on the east coast, McCaulou is the daughter of anti-gun parents who thought hunting was, at best, an odd hobby. McCaulou was a meat-eater, but didn't make the connection between a live animal and the packages of meat in the grocery store. Just out of college, she was working in the Indie film industry and living in downtown Manhattan when she decided to move west for a year or two.

She ended up in Central Oregon as a reporter at the *Bend Bulletin* and that's where we met. I was freelancing for the *Bulletin* at the time, after several years as a staff writer and photographer. McCaulou got my old beat covering La Pine and Sunriver.

9. *Snow Caves for Fun and Survival* by Ernest Wilkinson

Wilkinson is a former Search and Rescue member, and an experienced Colorado mountain guide, specializing in snowshoe treks and winter camping. This backcountry experience led Wilkinson to develop his own shelter-making techniques that save time and energy while also increasing comfort and safety. Igloo and lean-to construction are also discussed, as well as avalanche danger and how to avoid them.

10. *Staying Found: The Complete Map and Compass Handbook* by June Fleming

Any bushcrafter worth their salt should know how to use a map and compass. Forget GPS for long-term survival—any electronic device is only as reliable as the batteries in it. This book takes you from the basics of choosing a compass to advanced orienteering skills. It should be in every bushcraft and survival library.

11. *Desert Survival Skills* by David Alloway

Much of the American West is considered desert, and sometimes the towns are few and far between. Alloway, a veteran desert traveler, offers information on how to survive when stranded in a desert environment, focusing on the Chihuahuan and other North American deserts.

The book discusses survival priorities, emergency kits, water, fire, vehicle repairs and uses, plant and animal resources, tools and weapons, first aid, and other topics.

12. *Northern Bushcraft* by Mors Kochanski

The late Mors Kochanski is a legend in the wilderness survival field. His expertise spans well over fifty years. His specialty is survival in northern boreal forests.

This book provides practical advice on skills needed for extended stays in the wilderness, using a minimum of materials and tools.

Information included is on shelter construction, fire technology, proper care and use of axes, saws, and knives, and much more.

13. *A Reference Guide to Surviving Nature: Outdoor Preparation and Remedies* by Dr. Nicole Apelian and Shawn Clay

I have been following Dr. Nicole Apelian for years, on the reality series *Alone*, where she has appeared twice, and from reading her blog. I met her at Flintlock 2 in the Ozarks in June, 2019, and Apelian is as engaging in person as she is on TV.

In this latest publication, the authors cover the basics of emergency preparedness, including what gear you should carry on you. Learn the basics of fire, shelter, water, food, first aid, and signaling with this text. Various plant, insect, animal, and weather threats are covered, coupled with color photos for easy identification. Modern and natural suggestions for field medicine are also included.

Good fiction can teach and be a call to arms. And a good adventure book may get people thinking about the need for learning survival and preparedness skills. Here are several works of fiction to recommend to that person who might need a subtle nudge to start learning about preparedness.

14. *One Second After* by William R. Forstchen

This novel deals with an unexpected electromagnetic pulse attack on the United States as it affects the people living in and around the small American town of Black Mountain, North Carolina.

The realistic scenario and superb writing can provide a wakeup call to those people who scoff at the idea of preparedness for disasters.

15. *Alas Babylon* by Pat Frank

This 1959 novel was one of the first apocalyptic novels of the nuclear age and it is the first book of such ilk I ever read. Even as a teenager, the book grabbed and held my attention.

The novel deals with the effects of a nuclear war on the fictional small town of Fort Repose, Florida, which is based upon the actual city of Mount Dora, Florida. The title is derived from the *Book of Revelation:* "Alas, alas, that great city Babylon, that mighty city! For in one hour is thy judgment come."

Remember This:

The current state of the world makes it easy to get discouraged. Maybe you wonder what the point might be of preparing for emergencies. You're not alone, and historically, people have always prepared for the unforeseen. Joseph, in the Old Testament, had seven years of bounty, but he still prepared for a potential famine.

Today, the task may seem overwhelming at times. But start with little steps, and work toward a long-term goal of being ready for whatever emergency might come. Don't get discouraged—you've already taken some of the first steps by reading this far!

CHAPTER 2
DEVELOPING A SURVIVAL MINDSET

A survival mindset is necessary for enduring anything. It doesn't matter if you're in a wilderness environment, practicing bushcraft skills, or in a big-city, high-rise building when an earthquake hits. You must develop a survival mindset, and know how to use it if you intend to survive.

So, where do you start?

A good place is to understand what you're up against. Just what will you do if confronted with an emergency? How might you act? How will the people around you, most of them strangers, react?

This is knowable.

Preparedness is not a new science, and there is nothing new about the way people react to emergency situations. *Survival Psychology* by John Leach can help you understand what you may be up against during an emergency.

Leach studied survivors' reactions, including those of Union prisoners at the horrific Andersonville prison during the Civil War; to shipwreck survivors; to people who made it through plane crashes and natural disasters. Distilled down to one sentence, here's what Leach found: *Psychological responses to emergencies follow a pattern.*

One of my goals is to help you develop the survival mindset

needed to stay alive. Until you know what might happen in your mind, or in the heads of the people around you, there's no way to come up with a plan to survive.

So, we'll start with the baseline knowledge of what happens to people, mentally, in a survival situation. Survival situations bring out a variety of reactions—including some that make the situation worse.

Leach's studies show that only ten to fifteen percent of any group involved in any emergency will react appropriately. Another ten to fifteen percent will behave totally inappropriately and the remaining *seventy to eighty percent will need to be told what to do.* The most common reaction at the onset of an emergency is disbelief and denial.

Here's the typical disaster reaction progression, according to Leach:

1. **Denial:** The first reaction will probably be: "This can't be happening to me!" But an emergency, disaster, accident, or crash can happen to anyone, and it can put your life at risk. This disbelief causes people to stand around, doing nothing to save themselves. The eighty percenters in any survival situation will have to be instructed to help themselves.

2. **Panic:** Once you get past denial, there is a strong chance you may panic. This is when judgment and reasoning deteriorate to the point where it can result in self-destructive behavior. It can happen to anyone. To avert this problem, realize it may happen and use the STOP mindset exercise. (Explained in detail in the next section.)

3. **Hypoactivity,** defined as a depressed reaction; or **hyperactivity,** an intense but undirected liveliness: The depressed person will not look after himself or herself, and will probably need to be told what to do. The hyperactive response can be more dangerous because the affected person may give a misleading impression of purposefulness and leadership.

4. **Stereotypical behavior:** This is a form of denial in which victims fall back on learned behavior patterns, no matter how inappropriate they are for the situation. The Boss may decide to continue in that role, even though they have no idea of what to do. Sadly, the underlings may also revert to those subordinate roles, even though they may be better prepared mentally.

5. **Anger:** A universal reaction, anger is irrational. Rescue workers frequently come under verbal and physical attack while performing their duties.

    A few years ago in Central Oregon, the Deschutes County Search and Rescue team rescued a man who had dumped his raft just before going over a waterfall on the Deschutes River near Bend. Miraculously, the rafter saved himself by clinging to a mid-stream boulder. During the whole rescue effort, he denied he was in trouble. After being plucked from the rapids, the rafter flipped off the rescuers as he walked back to the parking lot. He never thanked anyone for saving his life.

6. **Psychological breakdown:** This could be the most desperate problem facing a victim, and this stage is characterized by irritability, lack of interest, apprehension, psycho-motor retardation, and confusion. Once this point is reached, the ultimate consequence may be death.

So, according to Leach, one key to a "survival state-of-mind" is to be prepared and confident that you can handle an emergency. This brings up another deadly behavior pattern: *lack of preparation.*

People don't prepare for emergencies, Leach writes, for three reasons: Planning is inconvenient, preparations may be costly, and an ingrained folk myth that says to prepare for a disaster is to encourage it.

I found this to be all too common in Central Oregon.

Flashback: A few years back, I was at Swampy Lakes Snow Park near Bend, getting ready for a snowshoe trek. An older couple pulled up next to me—tourists from the looks of their inappropriate clothing and rental equipment. They had no survival gear of any kind that I could see. They struggled to put their snowshoes on, then asked if there were any maps around. I gave them one of mine, and offered to orient it for them with my compass.

They declined.

They also didn't want the book of matches and a packet of fire-starter I tried to give them. And here comes the quote that keeps the Search and Rescue teams busy:

"We're just going out for a quick outing," the lady said. "We're not going to do any of that wilderness survival stuff."

She was absolutely right.

STOP and Keep from Panicking

Here's the scenario: You walked farther down that interesting-looking trail than originally planned and the sun is starting to set. An unsettled feeling in your stomach grows worse, and becomes a knot. The knot twists tighter as you look around. *Ohhhh, nooo*, you think. You may be lost . . .

Or,

You were walking up the stairs out of the subway, headed home from work, thinking about what to have for dinner. Then, there is complete darkness. Everyone around you on the stairs grows agitated. There is a rush upstairs and onto the street. The crowd of confused commuters mill around aimlessly. Nobody knows how to react, and your mind goes blank. Now what? Then, despite your best intentions, you feel yourself starting to panic . . .

Embed this in your psyche: STOP! Say it out loud if you have to, then remember what it stands for: *Stop, Think, Observe, Plan.*

This well-used old acronym, probably mentioned in every survival, bushcraft, or preparedness manual, is critical to your survival. STOP is a survival mind-set exercise. Here's how to use it, as explained by wilderness survival expert Peter Kummerfeldt. Follow these steps:

This event could turn into chaos in an instant if an earthquake occurred and the electricity went out.

1. **Stop:** Unless it's dangerous, quit moving and sit down. Breathe. Take a drink of water. Eat a snack. Stay put—you can't think until you can focus your thoughts. Time yourself—take at least thirty minutes to let the adrenaline wear off.

2. **Think:** Assess your choices and the tools available. Do you have your essentials and the necessary survival gear along? Can you use them? Knowing you're prepared for an unexpected night out, or that you have the tools to deal with the situation, can inspire self-assurance and ratchet down your fear. This confidence could keep you from doing something stupid.

3. **Observe:** Take the surroundings into account, because this will affect what comes next. Is it getting dark? Is the temperature dropping or is the weather getting bad? What can you anticipate happening in the immediate future? These environmental factors must be considered.

4. **Plan:** Based on your previous actions in this exercise, form an overall plan. Then make some immediate decisions and get going. Don't expect anyone to help you, and don't procrastinate.

Overcome Fear of the Dark

Flashback: In the mid-2000s, I worked as a reporter for the daily newspaper in Bend, Oregon where I frequently covered incidents of lost hikers and other rescue situations. During that period, I interviewed Sgt. Marvin Combs, former coordinator of the Deschutes County (Oregon) Search and Rescue, who told me this story:

A hiker kept walking all night, even though he was hopelessly lost in the Three Sisters Wilderness, a vast territory in central Oregon. In the darkness of the woods, the hiker didn't know the terrain and eventually his flashlight batteries wore out. He could easily have been injured in a number of ways by walking over a cliff or falling over a log or rock. Fortunately, the next morning he came out on a road, miles from where any searchers had been looking. He said he was afraid to stop and couldn't build a fire. So why did he keep moving?

"He told us, 'I heard animals or something moving all around me,'" Combs said.

In this case, fear of the dark could have led to disaster. So if you start to feel a little edgy and anxious as the sun goes down, don't let that affect later decisions you may have to make. The time to deal with that fear is before the survival situation develops. A standard

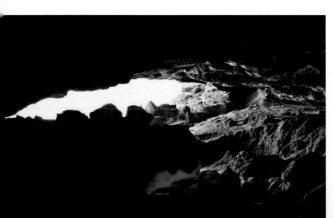

Find an area where you can control the amount of light and darkness, such as a cave or closet. Gradually start introducing more darkness, until you feel comfortable being in the dark.

bushcraft and survival skill is to identify a problem, and decide to overcome it. If you're afraid of the dark, don't think you're alone. Fear of the dark is called "nyctophobia." Sigmund Freud was one of the earliest researchers who made a study of this problem. He thought fear of the dark was an expression of separation anxiety.

In his book *Emotion,* William Lyons writes, "Fear of the dark is not fear of the absence of light, but fear of possible or imagined dangers concealed by the darkness."

Many, many adults are afraid of the dark, and some won't know it until all the lights go out. Think about it: The majority of city dwellers are never in complete darkness. Street lights, the ambient glow from stores and shopping centers, night lights in the house, and other illumination sources assure that there is never complete darkness. But suddenly, out in the woods, or in a building when the power grid goes down, darkness descends. If this causes uneasiness or fear, you might act irrationally.

Here is one suggested way to get over that fear. Psychologists call this "systematic desensitization." The idea is to confront the issue or problem in small, manageable steps and gradually desensitize yourself.

Here are some steps to take:

1. Realize the problem and decide to do something about it. Come up with some good reasons to conquer this fear. It could be that you have family responsibilities and would need to take care of others during an emergency.
2. Consider what might be causing that fear and give it a name, such as fear of wild animals in the dark. Research the possibility of animal attacks and decide if your fear is grounded in reality. Do this with any nameless fear—you can't overcome something if you don't know what it is.
3. Find a safe spot, outside if possible, that will get completely dark at some point, and go there. Sit down and observe the surroundings. Stay as the sun starts to set, and leave when you start to feel

uncomfortable. Do this regularly, extending the time you spend there. The goal is to be able to sit in complete darkness.

4. If you live in the city, you may have to go to your closet and regulate the light with the door and different-sized lights. (Don't do this without explaining the concept to the other residents!)

5. As you sit, listen and use your senses. Remember, the only difference between daylight and darkness is that you have lost your sense of sight. You can still listen, smell, and feel the wind or weather on your skin. Make this a sensory experience and concentrate on using all your senses.

6. Take up astronomy if that is feasible, and go look at the stars. Learn how to tell directions by the constellations, and learn some of the history of celestial navigation. An activity that requires darkness is a good way to take your mind off your fears.

7. I'm not afraid of the dark, but I don't like stumbling around in it, so there are always backup LED keyring lights in my pocket or attached to my coat zipper fob. Get a light that has an on-off switch, and preferably one that doesn't work when it is squeezed. Otherwise, it may inadvertently turn on when you don't want it to. This is bad news if the light is activated in your pocket and runs down the battery. The right keyring light can also provide about eight hours of illumination and may be enough to get you safely through the situation.

Overcoming a fear of the dark is nothing more than understanding why darkness makes you edgy, and then taking steps to become prepared. And everything done to increase preparedness for an unexpected emergency is a good thing!

Make a Plan to Survive

Flashback: "Why are we walking down the middle of the street?" my girlfriend asked. I didn't answer, being busy scanning the situation. I didn't let her hold my hand or take my arm. Up ahead, alongside the alley on the dimly lit, deserted street, a dark figure lounged. He was half-concealed in a door frame. Up ahead of him was another figure. This did not look good at all.

An urban survival situation can develop from an apparently harmless, routine activity. In this case, I took a date to a play and we were late leaving afterward. The performance had been at an obscure theater in a seedy, rundown section of Washington D.C. Leaving after the show, we took the wrong exit into the dead-end alley behind. The side door locked behind us before we could go back in. The scene before us was scary. The high-crime area was dimly lit by a street light, and there were all sorts of shadows and dark places on both sides of the street to conceal assailants. We started walking rapidly and my years of Taekwondo training kicked in.

I already had a self-defense plan, thanks to Dr. James Brockway, one of my Taekwondo instructors at Iowa State University. In class, we practiced multiple-attacker defense, and my intention was to maneuver any assailants into a one-on-one situation. Staying in the middle of the street eliminated any chance of a surprise attack.

As we drew even with the nearest person, I paused momentarily and he got the "Martial Arts Stare"—the one we practiced in sparring and for tournaments. It's a kind of dead-pan look that betrays no emotion, but is designed to project a confident, "Don't mess with me" attitude. After a moment, we resumed walking. The other figure looked away as we got near him.

Nothing developed from the situation, except a shaking in my knees!

Given a choice between traveling through a remote wilderness with wild animals, or a bad part of any big city, I'll take wilderness every time. But most of us live in urban areas, and nowhere is a survival mindset more important. Urban and wilderness emergency situations have many commonalities. A plan can help you survive either. And you are most likely to have to use your bushcraft skills in a big city or town.

During an emergency, plan on traffic being stopped on the highways. The infrastructure may be damaged, and the streets will be jammed with people fleeing the city.

So here's a possible scenario: *An earthquake hits while you're at work.* The office walls start to shake and the pictures begin to fall. Alarms go off. Heads pop up above the cubicles, as your co-workers, with no idea of what to do, look around. Some will sit back down and get back to work.

Now what? Stay? Go? Logout, then leave? Ignore the situation?

Knowledge is key to survival, and you are prepared. You never thought: "This can't happen to me." You paid attention at the mandatory safety meeting about building evacuation. You read earthquake survival information from the Federal Emergency Management Agency. Because of this preparation, you already have a survival mindset, a survival kit and a plan. You know where the stairs are, and the quickest way to get out of the building.

So, get out immediately. Ignore any jokes or jibes from the eighty percenters who don't have a clue of what to do next. Don't pay attention to the members of the ten percent who want to do something stupid. You are intent on survival, and that means getting out of the danger zone.

As I type this, I have a butane lighter in my pocket, a whistle, knife, fingernail clippers, LED flashlight, small knife, and magnesium stick on a belt clip, and a Swiss Army knife in my belt pouch. My wallet has firestarter, charcloth, and a signal mirror in it. This gear goes with me everywhere it's legal, even though the eighty percenters tend to roll their eyes if they notice my stuff. I have carried this collection in the pocket of a suit coat, or in my briefcase or daypack, but it's always with me.

Women can carry complete urban survival kits in their purses, and no one will ever be the wiser. After all, the earthquake could happen when you're in a meeting or away from your desk.

If the earthquake happens right now, and I have to sprint for the door and can't grab anything else, I have the minimum tools on me to make a fire and stay warm and signal for help.

In our office earthquake scenario, you may have to start using your survival tools immediately.

Here's how the evacuation situation could hopefully work out:

1. Your survival mindset clicks in and you leave your desk as soon as possible and head for the nearest exit. If necessary, push past the people who are starting to congregate and mill around. Grab the first-aid kit from the break room on your way past.

2. If the lights go out, then your flashlight makes you the leader. In the darkness, people will look toward the bright light and wonder what to do next. There will be people with cellphone lights, but these tend to be feeble and don't emit much light.

3. Blow your whistle loudly (this immediately makes you the perceived authority figure), and in a loud, matter-of-fact voice order everyone to remain calm and follow you quietly. (The eighty percenters still don't have a clue. They'll do whatever an authority figure tells them to.)

4. Your actions to organize an orderly evacuation may later win you a performance award and plaque from your company. *But*

the immediate purpose of this organization is to make sure *you* make it to the exit, and that's why you become the leader. If people panic, crowd around, or pile up around the door, nobody gets out.

5. Lead everyone in a quiet and orderly fashion down the stairs and out of the building. Don't let anyone or anything distract you. Your immediate goal is to get out of the building before it collapses.

6. Once outside, gather everyone at the rally point mentioned in the safety briefing, and then assess the situation. Order everyone to stay out of the building, and if someone insists on going back, order them to stay put.

Everyone is now responsible for their own safety, and you have accomplished your major goal: getting out of the danger zone.

If it is safe to do so, and there is no smell of gas or chemicals, building a campfire in a safe open area might be the next order of business. The fire will serve as a focal point, and a gathering place, as you wait for emergency personnel to arrive. Also, gathering firewood from pallets, dumpsters, etc. will give people a focus while they wait for rescue. Depending on the severity of the earthquake, what happens next is hard to determine. For now, you'll use the rest of your survival kit and training to make it through the emergency. This might mean you start walking home, or stay put and make a shelter to get people out of the elements. Someone may need medical attention. Find out who has taken a first-aid class and use the kit from the break room.

Now, you will need to use the rest of your bushcraft training and follow your "get home plan."

Why "Heading for the Hills" Won't Work

At virtually any bushcraft or preparedness event I go to, someone proclaims stockpiling food is a waste of money, and that when everything goes down, and society collapses, they will head out for the wilderness.

Their idea is that when a disaster strikes, everyone will have to fend for themselves. But these bushcrafters or survivalists will head for the wilderness and live off the land, apart from everyone else until the situation resolves itself.

That's what they think.

Here's the reality check: "heading for the hills" is impractical and foolhardy.

Here's five reasons why you shouldn't head for the wilderness:

1. Where will you go?

    Wilderness is in short supply in the United States. Both coasts are densely-populated, and there just aren't enough wilderness areas to go to during an emergency. Other wilderness or sparsely-populated areas, such as deserts and swamps, are uninhabited for a reason. Living conditions in some of these places would be too harsh for the average person to last long.

    That leaves private land, and good luck getting access to that. Farmers and ranchers will probably be unwilling to let hordes of city refugees squat on their land, and these rural folks are traditionally well-armed.

2. How will you get there?

    If you live near any major metropolitan area, it may be a several-hour drive under ideal circumstances just to get out of the city. (My record high commute home in Washington D.C. was six hours to go eight miles. And that was because of just one accident that jammed up the Beltway. In another instance, I got stuck on the New Jersey Turnpike for six hours because a crane had toppled over, blocking everything. It took another crane to remove it.)

    If the survival situation develops from a natural disaster like an earthquake, hurricane, tornado, or flood, the bridges may fail and roads may be covered with debris and thus be impassable.

Wilderness areas are remote, hard to get to, and not that commonplace. Chances are, the roads to these areas may be blocked or impassable.

Your carefully-packed vehicle may not even be able to get out of the garage.

If you can't drive on the roads, that leaves walking or some other alternative transportation. You will join hordes of unprepared people going somewhere. These crowds will be easy pickings for robbers or gangs.

And what about your gear? More than two-thirds of U.S. adults are overweight or obese, according to the Food Action and Research Center, and most Americans couldn't carry a loaded backpack anywhere. Can you realistically haul enough of your gear to effectively survive?

3. You think you're going to be the only one out there?

Flashback: It was the opening of elk season in the Idaho backcountry, several years ago, and there was almost a traffic jam at the trailhead. My hunting party was about twenty-five miles from the nearest town of Yellow Pine, Idaho, and there was one entry point into the Salmon Challis National Forest and millions of acres of wilderness.

Outfitters and hunters waited to unload and then park their vehicles. The situation seemed unreal; here we were, nearly fifty miles from the nearest highway, in the middle of one of the most isolated wilderness areas in the lower forty-eight, and parking was at a premium! My brother Mike counted fifty horse trailers.

As mentioned, the entry points of wilderness areas are crowded during opening days of hunting and fishing seasons. What will happen when thousands of refugees or unprepared people hit the roads and try to flee following some disaster?

There will undoubtedly be groups of unprepared people at these backcountry bottlenecks who will be depending on whatever they can beg or take from you.

4. Going camping is fun; survival living isn't.

Unless you're a hermit, an introvert who hates people, or just plain anti-social, the isolation of a faraway wilderness will soon become oppressive. People are social animals, which is why it's no coincidence that solitary confinement is used as a punishment in overcrowded prisons, or that loneliness is such an awful feeling.

After a few days or weeks of isolation, you'll probably be looking for other people just to have someone to talk to.

5. Living off the land?

Wild animals aren't stupid. Hunting pressure will either force them to leave the area, or they will be killed off to the point where they can't reproduce and replenish their population.

Responsible and regulated sport hunting and fishing guarantees that the wildlife populations can be sustained, and their habitat preserved. Unregulated killing will soon decimate or destroy some species of wild fish and animals.

There are reasons why we have hunting laws. During a catastrophic event, there will be scumbags who see their chance to slaughter game animals, or dynamite schools of fish. I don't foresee the game animals lasting long.

Besides, trying to maintain your body's needed caloric intake from fish or wild game meat is really, really hard. Just about any weight-loss diet has fish in it because it is a low calorie food. The same with foraged plants, tubers, and fruits. The big problem with foraging would be to avoid burning more calories than you harvest!

There are other reasons why this head-for-the-hills mentality isn't viable for most people. These are just the most obvious. Don't base your emergency survival plans on something that might not work. Do your homework now to come up with a practical disaster plan.

Ten Survival Items Apartment Preppers Need

Suppose you live in an apartment with limited storage space—what are some of the first things you need to be prepared for an urban emergency?

One reason I love the wild, open spaces of the West is because I was once an apartment dweller in downtown Washington D.C. After that experience of dense populations, jam-packed highways, and dependency on urban infrastructure, I can better appreciate clean air and wide open spaces. But I believe urban apartment dwellers should prepare for storms, floods, tornadoes, hurricanes, earthquakes, etc. too.

Even as a 1980s city dweller, I always had a backpack filled with camping gear, and it was ready to go on a moment's notice. We didn't call them "bug out bags" back then, and some people thought it was weird to have one!

But after several years in my first apartment, I realized an apartment-sized kit was needed. It had to be easily accessible for urban blackouts. So, I gathered supplies and packed them in a five-gallon, plastic bucket with a lid.

Suppose you live in an apartment in an area with the potential for natural disasters. (Which is everywhere!) Storage room is at a premium, but you can start collecting a few supplies for you to get by for a couple of days when the power goes out. Or if you have to evacuate from a tropical storm, hurricane, or flood warning, you'll quickly have what you need to throw in the car.

Here are some items that can make life a lot easier after a disaster:

1. **Five-gallon plastic bucket with lid:** This will serve as a storage container, a water bucket, or even an emergency toilet. In the case where the toilet still flushes, the bucket can be used to haul water to fill the tank. Many survival tools can be stored in the bucket until they are needed. Bottom line: every apartment needs a good bucket, but most don't have one.

2. **Spare batteries, extra toilet paper, and paper towels:** No brainer. You can compress paper towels and toilet paper for almost no weight with a big return. Remember, you may have to evacuate and people rarely remember toilet paper in the rush to get out.

3. **Backpacking stove:** A lightweight backpacking stove will give you a burner to cook food and boil water. Any stove that relies on a flame will produce carbon monoxide, so make sure the cooking area is adequately ventilated, next to an open window. Also, make sure there is a fuel supply easily available. For example, propane canisters may be hard to come by, whereas denatured alcohol may be easily found. Check out your local hardware, home improvement, and backpacking stores for potential fuel sources and stock up.

4. **Dehydrated food:** Include a three-day supply for each person. The shelf life on some of these foods is ten-to-fifteen years, so you don't need to worry about spoilage. Get the kind of dried foods that only need to have water added, and that don't have long simmering times. They make some pretty good meals these days. Look for ones that have no preservatives or additives.

5. **Crank cell phone charger:** I bought a simple crank charger for about fifteen dollars. It will recharge my cell phone and laptop, so communications can continue. Remember those scenes on

TV when Hurricane Sandy wiped out the Jersey shore and folks were paying big bucks to charge their cell phones at a local store? Don't be one of those people.

There are also some very efficient solar chargers and batteries on the market that can power anything from a phone to a television. I have several of these and as long as the sun is out, I can charge batteries.

As long as the sun shines, this solar panel can convert sunlight into energy, and can charge a phone, laptop, light, or any number of electric things.

6. **Crank or solar-charged flashlight:** Batteries wear out, so get a source of light that can be recharged. You'll have plenty of time when the electricity is out to keep the flashlight cranked up! Solar charged lighting tools or generators might be an option in some areas. There's a lot of solar technology these days that can power many of your needs for a few days.

7. **Candles and lamps:** Interior lighting might be a major problem, especially during the winter months when it starts to get dark at about five thirty in the evening. Hit the thrift stores and buy whatever candles they have. I keep packs of white, short candles and glass hurricane lamps to project the light. Kerosene or oil lamps are another option. Check out hardware stores for the small oil candles that burn for days. These lighting sources are incredibly reliable and won't break. If you need to loan a light to a neighbor during a power outage—and you will—some candles or a lamp will be greatly appreciated.

8. **Water storage containers and water filter:** If the power goes out, you'll need to store some water ASAP. I have been using the collapsible Platypus water containers for years, and they are reliable, durable, and compact. Get some of the collapsible five-gallon plastic jugs. Figure on a bare minimum of a gallon of drinking water per person per day. Better yet, fill up the bigger jug in advance of the event and put it in the bottom of your closet.

During a power blackout, your water quality might be suspect, so some sort of water purification method should be considered. There are many filters on the market, and the Sawyer filters have worked well for me. Boiling water is probably the safest way to purify it. Once the water is brought to boiling (212

Get water storage containers you can handle. Water weighs eight pounds per gallon. Make sure you can lift and pour from the filled container!

degrees Fahrenheit) for about a minute, everything that boiling temps can kill is completely dead.

Actually, bringing water to a rolling boil is enough. But remembering the one minute rule is easy and assures the water did get hot enough. Boiling water for extended periods of time doesn't make it hotter or cleaner. Once the water reaches 212 degrees, the temperature at which water boils, the water starts to vaporize. There are chemical water purification products that are easy for anyone to use—all you do is add them to water. I've used Polar Pure and Potable Aqua for years. Don't leave out this preparedness step—clean water is critical.

9. **Sleeping bag:** At night, a warm sleeping bag will allow you to sleep comfortably. Extra blankets are always a good idea. Use the power outage as an excuse to go camping in the living room with a loved one. It's a memorable adventure, good for stories that will last for years.

10. **Duct tape and Visqueen:** These are multi-purpose items. Duct tape is used for everything, and the large sheets of plastic Visqueen will allow you to cover a broken window, partition off a room, rig an emergency shelter, etc.

As a long-time prepper, this gear recommendation seems barely adequate to me. But this collection is an impressive start toward self-sufficiency for someone who is just starting out.

Where do you buy this equipment? Well, just look around, research on the Internet, and use this list to start your own search. Many useful items can be found at the local Tractor Supply, Lowe's, Bass Pro Shop, etc. Shop online today and have all this gear show up to your doorstep. Or have some fun and go down to your local military surplus store. Talk to the guy at the counter and browse around. Thrift stores are other good places to shop. I bought a like-new Coleman propane lantern at one for a couple of bucks, and it's not uncommon to find excellent camping gear and military surplus clothing.

It's your choice how to gather the supplies you need. But it's not a choice whether or not to do it.

Remember This:

Knowledge is the key to survival in any circumstance. If you are going to survive a desperate situation, developing a survival mindset beforehand is critical. You must be able to knowledgably assess a situation, understand what you are preparing for, and have a plan. This is a survival mindset.

Your survival mindset will help take away irrational fears of the unknown, and hopefully, allow you to function effectively in a crises situation. Don't read any further until you have figured out and set up your very own survival mindset. Without it, survival gear is not going to do you much good.

CHAPTER 3
MAKING A SURVIVAL KIT

Developing a survival mindset is critical. But you will also need some basic tools. These are called survival or emergency kits. They can range from small pocket or keyring kits, to full-blown, extensive collections of gear that are designed to last indefinitely.

The best kit for you is the one that you make. Remember that basketball dunk shot that most can't make? Well, that means there shouldn't be anything in the kit you don't know how to use too. Regular practice with your tools will assure you can use them during an emergency.

So let's get started.

The Ten Essentials and Stuff You Need

A very common question from bushcraft or wilderness survival new-comers is: "What gear will I need?"

And that's a really good question! Walk through any sporting goods store and you'll notice a bewildering array of gear, stuff, doo-dads, knick-knacks, and just plain junk. The educated buyer must decide which is which. Depending on what store it is, and the sales-person, you could end up buying some very expensive—and unnec-essary—items. In some stores, salespeople work on commission and push high-priced gear. Or you might end up with a clerk who is covering the counter for somebody at lunch. Now is a good time to read *Build the Perfect Survival Kit* by John C. McCann. This can give you some good ideas on where to begin, and help you decide how much gear you want to have in your kit.

So, here's a good place to start. The Boy Scouts of America have been preaching the gospel of survival common sense for more than one hundred years. I don't know who actually coined the term "Ten Essentials." But there is no question that a facsimile of this list is the basis of all emergency preparedness kits.

Here is a list of things you need, loosely based on suggestions from the Boy Scout Outdoor Essentials. Many of my gear suggestions below have been arrived upon after several years of different uses and applications. Look at these ideas, and then decide what will work best for you:

1. **Knife:** The best knife is up to your personal preference, but you must have some sort of cutting edge along. The *only* survival knife you have is the one you have along!

2. **First-aid kit:** A first-aid kit should go along on every outing, even if you never use it.

3. **Extra clothing and rain gear:** This will depend, of course, on the climate, time of year, and where you are. Clothing needs for a high desert area are much different than for those in the tropics. Since I trek through both deserts and swamps, my clothing will vary, depending on the location.

    You have essentially two choices for protection from the rain: rain suit or poncho. I use both, depending on the circumstances. I hiked the 225-mile John Muir Trail with a poncho for rain protection. It rained nine days straight! The poncho kept me dry, even though I was expending a lot of energy to hike.

    I prefer a rain suit while hunting, fishing, or canoeing because it won't flap in the wind, and because a rainsuit offers better protection while sitting or standing for long periods of time. Decide what you will be doing the most, and where you will be, to decide which type of rain gear will be best.

4. **Water bottle:** Water is an absolute necessity. I generally carry a Nalgene or other rigid water bottle to drink out of while outdoors. In my pack, I may carry several soft Platypus bottles to replenish my Nalgene. The soft bottle is protected in the pack and can be rolled up when empty. The softies weigh virtually nothing and take up very little space. And if you find a water source, and need to re-supply, you'll have ample containers along. Make sure to include some system of chemical purification or a water filter.

    I'm not a big fan of the water bladder systems. Their carry cases tend to be bulky and difficult to keep clean. They smell musty over time and have too many parts. But, the water bladder was great for my kids when they were young because they carried their own and the novelty of the drinking tube encourages sipping. It always kept them well-hydrated, even on long, hot desert hikes.

5. **Flashlight or headlamp:** I field-dressed a deer shortly after darkness fell one evening, holding my mini-Maglite in my teeth, like a cigar. Not having a headlamp was a major oversight on my part and the experience was pretty gross—talk about drooling. . . . Ever since that experience, I carry a good headlamp. A headlamp leaves your hands free if you are spelunking, or walking out to the car in the dark, scrambling over rocks, etc. Besides, if the lamp is on your head it is less likely to be dropped or broken.

A headlamp can free up your hands for other important tasks.

6. **Trail food:** In all my packs, I have several Clif bars, some jerky, sardines, and hardtack. The emergency food is fuel. You must have energy to stay warm and function, and that comes from the calories you digest.

Always carry nutritious, healthy snacks for quick energy, whether on your person or in your car.

7. **Matches and firestarter:** (Or other methods of ignition—you should have several different types.) I personally don't like matches at all for survival applications, but just about everybody knows how to light one. Firestarter will be worth its weight in gold when the tinder and wood are damp.

8. **Sun protection:** Sunscreen is an item that needs to be in every survival kit, regardless if you're in the arctic or the tropics. I carry the tube type, because it is less messy to apply. I generally carry Chapstick with sunscreen protection in it. The solid material is easy to apply to the nose, cheeks, and ears.

9. **Map and compass:** A GPS is also useful, but not without a map and compass! Get a solid baseplate compass and maps for the area you will be in and know how to use them. Always include spare batteries for your GPS.

10. **Shelter:** Tarp, garbage bag, bivy sack, etc. will all be useful. I always carry at least fifty feet of paracord or light rope, and four aluminum tent stakes.

This is my bare bones list, and you should expand and add categories to fit your individual needs.

An essential item on my expanded list is communications tools or items. How will you contact the local Search and Rescue people if you need help?

The first recommendation is to look at your cell phone. New cell phones have the E-911 chip that activates when 911 is dialed. This activation sends the position coordinates to the 911 dispatch center based on the phone's GPS system. The accuracy is reasonable.

The E-911 chip has helped to eliminate hours of searching and allows SAR volunteers to go straight to the subject. Older phones and some carriers may not have this capability. Check with your cell service provider and take another look if you use those inexpensive phones sold at the box stores. Remember, any cell phone must have connectivity with a cell tower to work.

Emergency dispatch call centers may have the option to "ping" your phone. This is essentially triangulating the hiker's position using a combination of a cell phone's signal and the cell towers. Multiple towers are best.

Accurate locating ability depends on the number of towers in the area. For example, Oregon's Mount Hood area has a lot of cell towers in the county adjacent to the mountain and surrounding forests. Multiple towers with the latest modifications provide accurate locating data. On the other hand, the ski resort at Mount Bachelor, Oregon, has only one tower. Subsequently, the position data is always suspect for those hiking on the Pacific Crest Trail west of that particular mountain.

While electronics are wonderful, consider carrying a signal mirror and a quality whistle. Though relatively inexpensive, these two components are key to finding lost hikers each year.

Make a Personal Survival Kit

Mention survival kits among recreationists and an argument/discussion will follow.

At one end of the spectrum is the guy who takes the heavily-loaded backpack full of gadgets, doo-dads, knick-knacks, and neat stuff. He may not go far, because of the pack's weight, but he'll be safe. Unless, one time, he decides to leave all that stuff at the car, since he's never used anything and its damned heavy. And he's just going a little way. . . .

Then he has become the optimist, the person at the other extreme. Since he has never been in an emergency situation, then it stands to reason that nothing will ever happen to him. There is no need for survival gear, since there has never been an emergency. And what's the point of preparing for some imagined disaster? There would be nothing he could do anyway. . . .

Somewhere between these extremes is the common sense approach.

Here's my take (and of course, this opinion may place me squarely in the survivalist wacko camp!): *Everyone should have a collection of survival tools with them at all times.*

I always carry several of these tools with me. These include a lighter, a small knife, whistle, LED light, and ferrocerium rod on a key ring, as well as firestarter, charcloth, and a signal mirror in my wallet. Be careful you don't forget you have the gear with you—you can't take even a tiny Swiss Army knife into a court room or through TSA at the airport.

All these items are commonly available and easily carried. Having them along could be a lifesaver. Suppose I have to run out of my house, right now. Let's say an earthquake (or wildfire, tornado, or flash flood) just hit and it is the middle of January. If I have to sprint for the door and can't grab anything else, I have the minimum tools on me to build a fire for me and neighbors, stay warm, help others, and signal for help.

If I can grab my jacket on the way out the door, there is an Altoids tin mini-survival kit in the pocket. And if I can get to my car there is a full component of survival gear in there, including food, water, a sleeping bag, and several tarps. I won't waste any time looking for equipment, when the walls may literally be falling down around me. This will come in handy for a quick evacuation due to a forest fire, urban natural gas leak, tsunami warning, or a forced evacuation of the neighborhood or city.

Any personal survival kit will ultimately boil down to opinion, knowledge, skill levels, and the season.

These survival items are easily carried. All my keys have a LED light attached. On my left key chain kit (from bottom, going clockwise) are belt clip, fingernail clippers, Swiss Army Knife, whistle, LED light, and ferrocerium rod. My keys, on the other ring, also have an LED light. Both lights have on/off switches.

Let's start here—many experts agree that a *minimum kit* should contain most of the following materials:

- **Survival knife:** This category covers a lot of ground, and personal preferences and prejudices have to be taken into consideration. Suffice it to say: any knife is better than no knife.

- **Fire making tool(s) plus fire starter:** Have a reliable ignition system you can use and some reliable firestarter. Making a fire during an emergency could be a lifesaver. Murphy's Law indicates that the more desperately a fire is needed, the more difficult it will be to start.
- **Navigation gear:** Get a quality, liquid-filled compass model that can be adjusted for declination. Have a map of the area, and GPS (with extra batteries), and mirror (for signaling).
- **Signal whistle:** Your voice will soon give out if you're calling for help. Anyone can blow a whistle. Get one that won't freeze, and that will carry for a long distance. (Want proof? Watch the movie *Titanic* again. The ship has gone down, and Kate Winslet is floating on a door. She is so cold, she can't yell for help as a rescue boat is going by. Blowing on her whistle is all that saves her.)

Always carry a pea-less whistle because it won't freeze while using it.

- **Flashlight:** This needs to be light, compact, and easy to use.
- **Shelter:** A tarp with paracord, a fifty-five-gallon trash bag, or a quilted, quality Space Blanket are good choices.

- **Food and water:** You'll want food and water, plus a water filter.
- **Clothing:** Having layers of fleece, wool, or polypropylene clothing will allow adding or subtracting pieces to stay comfortable. A waterproof packable shell jacket rounds out your minimum kit.

While commercial survival kits are available, the quality of some items is suspect. Some things, such as fishing hooks, sinkers, and line are included because people think they need them. And some items are included in commercial kits because they're cheap and take up space.

Start with a realistic assessment of your skills and needs, then start researching. A survival kit that works in the cold winter of Oregon, for example, will have different equipment requirements than one designed for Florida, and vice versa.

The idea is to make your own bushcrafting survival kits. Commercial kits may include cheap and worthless things in them to keep the cost down. The components in my pocket-sized Altoids tin kit would cost about fifty to sixty dollars to replace. My life is worth that to me!

Ask yourself these questions to get started making your personal survival kit:

- **Can I dunk a basketball?** You've read this analogy before. Point being—just because you've seen some bushcrafting skill done, doesn't mean you can do it. Apply this analogy to any survival technique.
- **Do I know anything?** Be honest! It doesn't matter how much survival gear you have, it's worthless if you can't, or don't know how, to use it. Take a good look at your skills and abilities, and face your inadequacies.
- **Will I make a commitment to learn?** Again, be honest, and don't put this off. If you don't know how to use a map and compass, perform first aid, or make an emergency shelter, learn now. Sign up for a community college course, read good survival books, and talk to the folks, like the Search and Rescue people, who are

actually using these skills. If a disaster happens this afternoon, maybe all you will have to work with is what you've got.

- **What gear is practical?** I was an assistant scoutmaster of Boy Scout Troop 18 in Bend, Oregon for seventeen years. Over that time, I noticed a lot of "survival gear" that is nothing more than expensive junk. Talk to someone in the know, and find out what urban or wilderness survival gear they use. Assess those items with your skill level and then decide what you need.
- **Will I make a commitment to carry this survival kit with me?** The best gear in the world does you no good if you don't have it with you. Your survival kit must be compact and convenient to carry or it will get left behind.

Here are a few suggestions, once you've made a survival kit commitment:

- **Can you use everything in the kit?** Using some suggested items may be beyond your skill levels. Your choice is to learn how to use everything or replace that particular component.
- **Don't let your survival kit give you a false sense of confidence.** Gear doesn't replace knowledge.
- **Consider if you have specific medical needs or conditions.** Make sure the kit includes the appropriate medications.

Every community has a survival guru with a website, but that doesn't mean they know anything. In fact, be leery of *any* survival website— a lot of posers are out to make a fast buck. Start learning by contacting the people who work with emergencies every day: police, sheriff's, and fire departments, Search and Rescue, the Red Cross, etc. and see if they have gear recommendations. They will also have a pretty good idea of who is a good teacher and who is a charlatan.

Finally, apply your common sense filter to anything associated with survival. Beware of bushcrafting or survival expert websites, TV shows, and articles. View any information with your eyes open. If your BS alarm starts to go off, there is probably a good reason for it. Then, educate yourself. Practice with your survival tools. Don't take any recommendations at face value unless the source has been proven to be reliable. Then, make your survival kit and take it along.

Every time.

What a Mini Kit Can't Do

Several years ago, the newspaper I worked at tasked me to write a practical winter survival guide for Central Oregon. It was an investigative reporting assignment, and I interviewed local experts from the Deschutes County Search and Rescue, as well as local survival equipment tester, the late Jim Grenfell, and internationally-known survival expert Peter Kummerfeldt.

The end result of months of research and testing was a system that included a personal, pocket-sized kit as well as a complete backpack setup for hardcore winter survival. But why carry a smaller kit on your person, when there is the complete Ten Essentials and extensive bushcrafting gear in your backpack, on the pack horse, in the car, or in the canoe?

Here is why.

Flashback: My wife, Debbie, and I are experienced canoeists, and we were on a family float trip on the John Day River in north central Oregon. The Clarno rapids last about three-quarters of a mile, and we had pulled up on shore to assess that stretch. We had just about decided to portage around the whitewater. Then a group of two canoes passed us, and they headed down the rapids. The paddlers were good—it didn't appear that any of the canoes got a drop of water in them. So, Debbie and I reasoned, we are experienced and competent canoeists. We should be able to follow their path, and run the rapids too.

Remember that basketball dunk shot?

We managed to hit a rock crossways right at the head of the rapids, and we were both thrown out of the canoe. We were wearing life jackets, and both of us knew what to do in that sort of situation. I righted myself, pointed my feet downstream and tried to follow the course originally set for the canoe.

Debbie, paddling up front, was in the water just ahead of me. Her head bobbed above the rapids as she navigated the whitewater. Several minutes later, I pulled myself out in the slack waters of an eddy. From downriver, Debbie waved to show she was okay.

Picking my way over the rocks toward her, I did a mental inventory of my survival tools. Everything we had, all of our fishing, camping, and survival gear, was headed downstream toward the Columbia River. It was a hot day, with no danger of hypothermia, and the other members of our float party were at the scene. Neither of us were injured, and it was not a survival situation. But if we had been alone, here's the survival tools we had left: I didn't lose my hat, glasses, or the GPS in my left shirt pocket.

However, the Mora knife was gone from its sheath on my belt, and the butane lighter in my left front pants pocket had disappeared. A whistle was attached to my life jacket. I had charcloth in a plastic bag, firestarter, and a ferro rod on my key ring survival gear. Debbie had a whistle, too, but her survival gear was somewhere downstream. Even soaking wet, we could have started a fire to warm up and signal for help. Downstream, the group of expert canoeists saw our canoe float by and snagged it. I lost four fishing rods, two tackle boxes, and everything that wasn't tied down.

You could fall out of a canoe, get thrown off a horse, be in a vehicle accident, etc. and end up separated from your gear. The only equipment available may be what is in your pockets.

But!

There is a real danger with any survival kit. That kit may give a false sense of security and self-confidence. A beginner may think the kit is a substitute for learning important survival skills.

The worst danger, in my opinion, is that a person will pick up a commercial mini kit, toss it in the daypack, and never learn how to use the components. Then, during an emergency, the kit may prove to be inadequate.

This is a typical pocket kit. (The item inside the tin is a reflection from the studio light!) 1. Cordage 2. Compass 3. Ferrocerium rod wrapped with jute twine 4. Signal mirror 5. Petroleum jelly 6. Charcloth 7. Can opener 8. Pocket kit tin 9. Firestarter 10. Wire 11. Utility blade 12. Rubber bands (for holding the tin shut) 13. Medications 14. LED light 15. Whistle 16. Swiss Army Knife

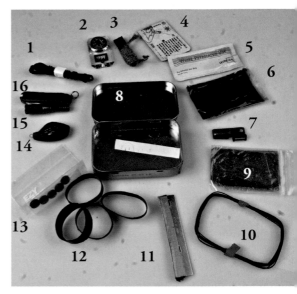

Here are five things a mini kit *can't* do:

1. **Save your life:** No survival tool, or collection of gear, can save you. You will save yourself, and you can't rely on anyone else or a single piece of equipment.
2. **Be your only survival gear:** A tiny, pocket-sized survival kit is a bare minimum selection for survival. At best, it is better than nothing. Carry a full-blown, complete Ten Essentials kit as part of your everyday carry.
3. **Replace skill and training:** Training and experience trumps equipment every time. You must practice with every piece of equipment in your kit. If you can't use an item or it doesn't work, discover that while testing it in your garage, not during an emergency.
4. **Be a long-term survival solution:** You can't rely on any kit for a long term solution to a flood, earthquake, or other natural disaster. Long-term survival requires long-term prior planning.

5. **Replace pre-planning:** Think about bushcrafting and how it can relate to wilderness and urban survival. Little things can make a big difference.

Assemble a Bug-Out Box for Your Vehicle

Generally, your best bet may be to stay home if there is some sort of disaster. Typically, all the roads away from a disaster scene will be jammed, and there may be gridlock on the highways, with nobody going anywhere.

Or, there might be a tree down across the driveway that prevents you from going anywhere, or even getting out of the garage. Or the bridge down the road may be out. Fleeing to safety might not be possible.

But what if you have to evacuate? There might be a hurricane or flood coming, and your area is ordered to be evacuated. What if you are away from home, and have to get there. What survival tools should you have in your vehicle?

Here are ten things you should carry in your vehicle:

1. **Survival mindset:** "It will never happen here," and "If something bad does happen here, there will be nothing I can do about it" are common mindsets that get people killed. The first obstacle to overcome are these attitudes.

   Long before the disaster strikes, be thinking about what you might need to do. Get the family involved to come up with a survival plan. Choose someone reliable out of the area as a contact point. Then, should the group be separated, everyone would know to contact that responsible person.

   Make sure everyone knows to check in with the Red Cross if they get separated from the group.

2. **Maps and a compass:** A GPS may be worthless in some areas. You might end up lost in the dark, with no idea of where to go. Learn how to use a map and compass to stay found.

   Get the right maps. A standard state road map is really useful, but usually doesn't have the details needed to figure out alternate routes around traffic jams. City and county maps may show lesser-known routes around disaster areas, and fire road maps will show every road. These detailed maps could prove invaluable for avoiding traffic jams or gridlocked areas.

3. **Cash:** When the power grid goes down, as it did during Hurricanes Harvey and Irma, that means ATMs won't work. With no power, you can't use a debit, credit, or cash card to buy gas or groceries. During a power outage, everything goes on a strictly cash basis. Have a cash reserve on hand, and a way to carry it safely and unobtrusively. Make sure you have enough money to get you through several days. Take twenties and smaller bills. Larger bills may not be accepted, or you might not be able to break them or get change.

4. **Games and toys for kids:** The novelty of evacuating will soon wear thin for kids and most adults, and their electronic devices will eventually run out of juice. Some simple board games that everyone can play in the car or at camp will be invaluable. A couple decks of cards can be the basis of virtually unlimited entertainment. Books are nice to have along, too.

5. **Flashlights and batteries:** No brainer here. There probably won't be functioning street lights, and you will have to provide any needed light. Get everyone a couple of the keychain LED lights to use in the car, or for going to the bathroom in the dark. Make sure they have on-off switches, and won't inadvertently turn themselves on in your pocket. These tiny lights are invaluable, and I use them a lot in hunting camps.

    Find several reliable lights and have a lot of batteries. For most activities, you won't need a 300 Lumen torch, but you do need a couple for checking out road conditions, viewing things in the distance, etc. I always carry a headlamp, so if a tire has to be changed in the dark I can have both hands free.

6. **Shelter and clothing:** While you can shelter in your vehicle, this is not ideal, especially after you've spent all day driving in bumper-to-bumper traffic. Take a small tent, sleeping bags, and tarps to create a camp as needed. Include seasonally appropriate clothing such as layers for warmth, rain gear, snow coats, snow boots, or walking shoes. Always include a backpack in your

automobile. There are times when you may choose to walk out or walk home and carry supplies with you.

Always carry in your trunk a rug and tarp for changing the tire, a good tire iron (not the poorly designed irons that come with the car), and headlamp for keeping your hands free.

7. **Gas cans:** Gasoline is life during an evacuation, and chances are, it will be scarce. Get some gas containers you can personally handle, and if possible, fill them up before you hit the road.
8. **Food and water:** Another no-brainer. Assume there will be nothing available. Have some food along that doesn't require refrigeration, and several water containers that are sturdy and can be refilled. I use the Platypus collapsibles a lot—they are rugged and can be rolled up when not in use, saving a lot of space.
9. **Electronic charging devices:** Cell phones and other communication electronics may or may not work. If you can't recharge them, they are guaranteed not to work! Give some thought to getting a charging station, a solar charger, or a battery that can be recharged. You may be able to communicate through texting,

This battery can be charged with a solar panel and then can charge other electric devices.

and you never know when the phone might suddenly decide to work again.

10. **Medical, tax, and other personal records:** When evacuating your home, be prepared to quickly gather your important personal papers by having them already organized in a school-style, zippered 3-ring binder or a waterproof container. These need to be on paper and sealed in a waterproof container. Keeping all your records on a CD, ZIP drive, or thumb drive is a fine idea, but, again, there must be power for them to be read. Also, first responders may be leery of inserting a strange drive into their computers for fear of a malware virus.

Most people forget that Hurricane Katrina knocked out all services and infrastructure on the gulf coast of Mississippi for weeks. Hurricane Harvey forced thousands to quickly evacuate Houston. During 9/11, people in New York walked for miles over the bridges to get home. The 1989 Loma Prieta earthquake in California killed dozens of people, and caused bridges to collapse and infrastructure to fail. Countless tornadoes destroy communities in the Midwest and Southern states every year. Every community in America is one natural disaster away from complete city-wide devastation. When your car includes a fully stocked "bug out box," you now have choices to either shelter in place, evacuate to a safe zone, or walk home with the needed survival supplies.

If you have chosen to own a firearm and you're in compliance with the law, you may want to include a weapon as well.

Make a Dutch Oven Survival Kit

The best cooking tool for preppers, survivalists, campers, and foodies of all types is the cast iron Dutch oven.

Flashback: Hurricane Katrina was due to hit land in a few hours, and my relatives in Mississippi, about 150 miles north of New Orleans, were not sure what was going to happen. I overheard my wife talking on the phone to her sister, Patti, of Clinton, Mississippi. In the middle of the hurricane preparation discussion, they started talking about recipes and what to cook using a cast iron Dutch oven!

Everyone near Katrina faced a potential power outage that could last indefinitely. There was a discussion of evacuating, versus staying put. Regardless, among the urban survival necessities in *any* natural disaster is a way to cook and purify water by boiling.

We had given Patti a hand-me-down cast iron camp oven with a lipped lid and three legs. Designed to be heated on top and bottom with campfire coals or charcoal, the camp oven was considered a necessity on the American frontier for at least two centuries.

This type of oven was taken on the 1803 Lewis and Clark expedition, was used by travelers on the Oregon Trail, and was indispensable in countless cabins, lean-tos, and soddies. Technically, a "Dutch" oven has a rounded top, no legs, and can be used in a conventional oven on top of a stove, or on an outdoor propane fish cooker or grill.

For hundreds of years, cast iron has set the standard for utility, durability, even cooking and taste. Today, one of the best and most important preparedness items you can buy is a cast iron camp oven. I've been cooking with Dutch ovens at hunting and fishing camps

A camp oven can be used outdoors under extreme circumstances.
Metal dog food pans allow
Dutch ovens to be used
safely.

A typical metal pan can be
turned upside down on a
charcoal chimney lighter to
shield the coals from the
rain.

for decades, and on many camping trips and Boy Scout and Girl Scout outings. For years, I taught the course for the BSA cooking merit badge.

I'm here to tell you—this simple utensil can fry, bake, sauté, or boil any food that can fit inside. During an emergency, a Dutch oven can cook or boil water, fueled by just about anything.

So, you may be wondering: What do I need to get started with Dutch oven cooking?

My wife's advice to her sister was to get at least fifty pounds of charcoal and three round, fourteen-inch diameter metal pet food dishes. Put the oven, these items, and some basic cooking utensils in a square milk crate for storage.

Here is the basic, bare-bones list of Dutch oven survival kit necessities. They are all you need:

- **One twelve-inch Lodge brand shallow cast iron oven:** I like Lodge cast iron, because it has a proven quality record. Camp Chef makes a good product, and several experienced Dutch oven cooks I know prefer that brand. Choose what you like, but be careful as you'll get what you pay for. A cheap, poorly-made oven won't work particularly well, and you'll probably end up replacing it with a quality piece. Sometimes I take an aluminum oven on outdoor excursions, instead of cast iron, to save weight.
- **Three shallow metal pans with lipped rims:** These are critical, and common dog or bird food pans work very well. Put one pan underneath the oven to protect the coals from dampness and to help regulate heat; and use another pan to store lit coals. The third is a spare that is used to cover the oven and protect it from rain or snow while cooking.
- **One lid lifter:** In a pinch, a pair of channel lock pliers will work.
- **One trivet or tripod:** This is a wire or metal rack that holds the lid while you stir the contents of the oven or adjust seasonings. It keeps the lid clean and out of the dirt.
- **One knife:** You probably don't need a tactical or survival knife, but you will need something that will work for food preparation.
- **One nylon spatula:** This is used for cooking and cleaning the oven.
- **One large nylon spoon:** This is used for stirring and serving the food.
- **Source of heat:** Charcoal is easy to use, and provides an easy method of regulating heat. Make sure you have an adequate supply!

The lid lifter, trivet, survival knife, spatula, and spoon all fit inside the oven. (If they don't, trim the handles.) All these items fit into a nylon commercial Dutch oven holder. Another great way to carry everything is in a square milk crate. Put the metal pans on the bottom, and the oven won't tip over. The loaded crate stacks nicely.

Cleaning a Dutch oven is easy. Take the spatula, scrape out any food residue, and fill it with water. (Never put cold water into a hot oven. It might cause it to crack.) Put the oven back on the coals and boil the water. Usually this will be enough to clean the oven, and all that remains is to scrape out the softened food debris and wipe it dry. Wipe down the cast iron with a light film of oil to protect against rust.

Obviously, there are other "nice-to-have" cooking items that could be included. But this basic Dutch oven survival kit will get you by in a wilderness or survival situation.

Remember This:

Once a survival mindset is established, the next step is to make sure the correct tools are at hand. No survival gear will do you any good if it isn't easily accessible, or if it is stored where it can't be used. Make your own survival kits of items that will be useful to you. These kits can range from items worn as part of your wardrobe, to collections that fit in daypacks, satchels, or brief cases, to full blown survival kits that are carried in your vehicle.

Knowing how to use these items is critical, and there is no substitute for practice.

CHAPTER 4
CHOOSING CLOTHING

Your clothing is your first line of defense against hypothermia and hyperthermia. But there are many aspects about clothing that will determine how effective it can be for protecting you. Here are some clothing suggestions for staying cool or warm.

Pick the Right Clothing Fabrics

Make sure the fabrics in your clothing will keep you comfortable and not be hazardous to your health!

Different fabrics have radically different properties. Choosing the wrong type or mixing clothing of different materials can be disastrous. I didn't come up with this idea. The ancient Hebrews figured this out in the book of Deuteronomy (22:11) which states, "Do not wear clothes of wool and linen woven together," (New International Version).

During the Civil War, the South was desperate for wool to make uniforms, so they sometimes mixed cotton fibers with wool. It would be hard to imagine a worse material for hard-use outdoor wear! The fabric combined the worst attributes of either fiber.

Wool holds in heat when damp—which is not a good thing in the subtropical climate of the Deep South. Cotton holds in moisture. The end result was a material that was hot and slow to dry. The material was called "shoddy," and it didn't work well.

The Merriam-Webster dictionary defines shoddy as, "cheaply imitative, inferior, shabby, or disreputable."

When you are shopping for bushcraft or survival clothing, you may not be able to tell the properties of a garment just by looking at it. A nice, fuzzy, and thick one hundred percent cotton flannel shirt will be warm and cozy until it gets wet. At that point, the wet shirt may suck the heat out of your torso and cause hypothermia!

On the other side of the equation is wool. My hands-down favorite in the winter is clothing made with one hundred percent wool. But this may not be the best choice for a desert hike in August. Wool breathes well, and while it provides some UV protection, the material prevents your body from cooling too quickly.

That said, the desert tribes who roam the Rub' al Khali (otherwise known as the Empty Quarter, on the southern Arabian Peninsula) have for generations worn clothing uniquely designed for the harsh climate. In the largest sand desert in the world, daytime temperatures regularly hit the triple digits while nighttime temps can drop into the low fifties, and frosts have been recorded.

I was dressed completely in wool to shovel out my driveway after an Oregon snowstorm. I wore this same outfit while building igloos and camping in the winter.

The basic "dress" for the desert tribes is a tob or thobe of (usually) white cotton to the ankles. Over this, a sleeveless coat is worn that may be made of camel wool and often features stripes when worn by Bedouins.

Before buying any clothing item, read the labels and discover the material content. Ignore fashion or what's trendy (I know that's hard—I have a daughter who likes to stay updated with the current fashions) and make your purchase based on the activity and the clothing protection that will be needed. That includes the sun protection factor (SPF) rating of a good all-around summer shirt.

Top Fabric Choices for Outdoor Clothing

Cotton: Depending on where you live, cotton clothing can kill you. Cotton is "hydrophilic," meaning it is no good at wicking wetness away from the skin, and can become damp just by being exposed to humid air.

Once wet, cotton feels cold and can lose up to ninety percent of its insulating properties. Wet cotton can wick heat from your body twenty-five times faster than when it is dry. What feels like a cool and breezy shirt to you in the hot sun can quickly become dangerous if it cools below sixty degrees at night and your clothes are still wet. In humid conditions, it is hard for a cotton shirt to dry.

People have died from hypothermia in the middle of summer when caught overnight in wet clothes. Ergo, warm areas are not safe from hypothermia. According to Florida's Office of Vital Statistics, there were 249 direct temperature-related deaths from 1979 through 1999 in the state, based on the latest information available. Of these deaths, 125 were from excessive heat and 124 were from excessive cold. The number of temperature-related deaths during this period is greater than those from hurricanes, tornadoes, and even lightning.

But that doesn't mean that cotton isn't a fine option sometimes. I spend a lot of time in the Deep South, and my favorite hot weather shirt is a medium-weight, white, one hundred percent cotton Navy Surplus shirt. My favorite shirt has a thick collar that can be pulled up to shade my neck, and pockets with flaps and buttons. Cotton also has a modest amount of ultraviolet radiation protection.

You can buy a plain, affordable white twill short sleeve shirt and wear it for years around the pool, beach, during water sports, fishing, or any other activity. Just throw it in the wash with bleach. When it gets too stained to wear, buy another one.

On really hot days in a canoe, a cotton shirt can be soaked with water, and worn to prevent heat-related problems. On a hot desert trek, use a few ounces of water to wet the shirt down. The water can come from anywhere, and doesn't have to be clean, as it is just to be used for evaporation.

If you must conserve water in an emergency, pee on your shirt to wet it. Just make sure to have another dry shirt along to change into when needed. Once the cotton shirt gets wet, it is not going to be warm. You could end up in trouble if that is your only shirt when the temperature drops.

Don't be misled by the looks and camouflage patterns of one hundred percent cotton outdoor clothes. These garments may be just fine for a hot September dove hunt in the Deep South, or unseasonably warm deer hunt in November, but they become cold and clammy when damp or wet. And after sundown you could be mighty uncomfortable. I recommend a wool or polyester blend for this type of clothing.

Polypropylene: This material doesn't absorb water, so it is "hydrophobic." This makes it a great base layer, since it wicks moisture away from your body. Athletes swear by it since they need to get the sweat off the body as fast as they work it up.

For outerwear, there's poly fleece, but it's not really that warm, unless used as an under layer. It tends to be pretty loosely woven, so the wind can cut through it fairly easily. The bad news is that polypropylene is made from plastic which melts, so a spark from the campfire may put holes in your clothing and burn your skin.

My wife had a nice Columbia fleece jacket that was ruined by campfire "pops." Polypropylene also retains body odor, in my experience, and shirts can stain badly under the arms. Keep this fabric as your under layer on the ski slopes, during a marathon, or when participating in other active sports events. But I don't like the material for camping or light hiking.

Polyester: This is essentially fabric made from plastic, and it is quality stuff for keeping you toasty warm. The material has good insulating and wind stopping value and can be made into many different thicknesses.

I used a fiberfill sleeping bag on my 1980 end-to-end canoe voyage of the Mississippi River, and the bag always kept me warm, even when wet. Polyester is great for a lightweight overcoat that repels moisture.

My kids wore these kinds of rain jackets all the time growing up in Central Oregon. Many running shirts are loose-weave polyester and will wick away moisture while providing a windbreak against the chest. But the shirts tend to stain under the arms, and oil stains won't come out. My wife has ruined several polyester sport golf shirts while cooking in the kitchen.

Nylon: The fabric is pretty tough and can be used as your outer layer. It doesn't absorb much moisture, and what it does evaporates quickly. Nylon is best used as a windbreaker fabric, to keep your clothing from being compromised by wind and light rain. Nylon is a great fabric for a poncho and I keep one packed in all my survival packs.

Wool: When I lived in Central Oregon, wool was my standard go-to fabric for six months of the year. When I was an assistant scoutmaster with Boy Scout Troop 18 in Bend, Oregon, the first clothing we recommended new scouts buy was a good pair of wool pants and wool socks. For our winter camping excursions, any sort of cotton clothing is strongly discouraged, and jeans are outright banned from camp. You will not go wrong wearing wool during your winter activities.

Wool absorbs some moisture, but stays warmer than most all other fabrics, even when wet. It's comfortable even during a rainy or snowy day. Sure, you might get damp wearing a beanie, gloves, scarf, or sweater, but you won't be cold. This protection from the cold is critical in an emergency situation if you're caught out in the rain or snow, or if you fall while hiking across a stream. Wool is also inherently flame retardant, so warming up by a fire is less dangerous than when wearing other fabrics.

Silk: I've gotten positive feedback about one hundred percent silk garments from skier friends. I'll confess that I've never worn silk layers, as they are a bit over my budget and not part of my paradigm. But silk makes sense. Silk is a natural fabric, not bulky, and it makes a thin underlayer of insulating comfort. It has been worn for ages in Europe.

Down: This material is not a fabric, but rather fluffy goose down and feathers stuffed inside a garment or sleeping bag. When dry, down is one of my favorite insulating materials. But I don't use a down sleeping bag and would hesitate wearing a down vest into the back country because of potential moisture problems. When wet, down becomes hydrophilic, and loses virtually all its insulation value. It can be worse than cotton as far as sucking heat away from your body.

In addition, a down sleeping bag or garment is virtually impossible to dry out in the backcountry, even with a roaring campfire. Down is wonderful for the urban town scene to keep you warm when shopping or going out for coffee. I know experienced outdoorspeople who swear by down, but it's not my choice for serious outdoor activities.

Today, more than ever, we have an abundance of options in all kinds of traditional and hi-tech fabrics to help us enjoy the outdoors. Be prepared for any weather and any emergency by knowing your fabrics—and have a great time.

Find the Best Outdoor Hat

Follically-challenged guys like me require head protection. And you should too. But not just any head covering or hat is going to work. Your hat choice depends on the climate, environment, and temperatures.

The hat choice for the hot desert may not work well at all in a snowy cold environment. So start shopping for that outdoors hat with an idea of where it will most likely be worn.

We'll start with the brimmed, uninsulated hat that is going to offer the best protection from the elements, from freezing temperatures on up. My vote goes to a broad brimmed—say 3½ inches wide—wool fedora. A fedora style hat has been my choice for decades of outdoor activities, and I will explain why soon.

But first, here are some hats that don't make the cut for me:

Baseball-style caps: On my 1980 end-to-end canoe voyage of the Mississippi River, I wore an Iowa State University trucker-style baseball cap. The wind on the river would blow off any wide-brimmed hat, and I had a lot more hair back then for protection.

But these caps only shade your eyes, and offer little to no protection from rain or sun on your face. Hunt or hike in the rain wearing one, and you'll learn how uncomfortable it is to have water running down your neck.

Besides, on guys like me with a big, square head, baseball hats look dorky. My hiking partner, John Nerness of Los Gatos, California has a small head. Any baseball cap looks great on John, and they all appear to have been designed for him. If looks are important, make sure the baseball caps work for you.

That being said, I wear a trucker hat when I'm going to be in and out of a vehicle, or where it is bound to be windy. The baseball caps do protect that growing bald spot on my head! If you are wearing a raincoat with a hood, a trucker hat will help keep the hood's material from obstructing your vision.

And there are baseball-style hats that have an attached piece of fabric that shades the neck and ears. These can be a viable option.

Floppys: The short-brimmed, floppy hats like Gilligan wore are not much good, in my honest opinion. The brim is too short to shield your eyes from the sun's glare, and the rain can drip down the low spots in the brim. They are better than a baseball cap, but not by much. Many service members wear boonie hats as part of their uniforms.

Fedora Style Brimmed Hats

According to the Village Hat Shop: "From the late 1890s to the 1950s, the fedora was *the* hat to have for men. With an indented crown and characteristic "pinch" near the front on both sides, this hat style is pretty instantly recognizable. Whether wide or short brim, made of wool felt, straw, or leather, this classic hat truly stands the test of time."

My first felt fedora was a hand-me-down from my dad. It was a Stetson he wore when dressing up. I wore Dad's hat on several major backpacking trips until it virtually disintegrated.

That Stetson was on my head when I hiked the John Muir Trail. The constant rain in the Sierras, interspersed with brilliant sunlight at high elevations, made me appreciate the protection.

Based on decades of wearing experience, here is what I look for in an outdoor hat:

Wide enough brim: A brim of the proper width will keep rain off your neck and sun off your face.

Put the hat on, and see where the drip line would hit you. The rain will drain off the hat, and I prefer that the brim directs the moisture to hit about the middle of my back. In heavy rain, I will be

My brother, Michael Pantenburg, wore a wool, broad-brimmed hat on a backpacking trip in the Colorado Rocky Mountains. The chin strap was needed when we hiked across the Great Divide and a storm came up.

wearing a poncho or rain suit, and the water will be directed away. If the brim is too wide, it will hit against your daypack. Then check to see if the brim shades your eyes well. This becomes a big deal in the higher elevations of the mountains, or in the desert, where the sunlight is intense.

Chin strap: Think about adding a chin strap if there is the potential for high winds. Gale force wind is a big deal on the Mississippi River, where I am a canoe guide. The wind gusts upstream and the force will blow any hat off your head if it is not secured. That happened to me at Lake Powell, Arizona. I was on the deck of a cruise ship, when a single, unexpected gust blew my favorite Pendleton fedora off my head and into the lake.

Material to fit the situation: A black felt cowboy hat may not be the best choice in the blazing desert, nor do you want a mesh-crowned jungle hat in a snow storm. And a well-ventilated straw is the traditional choice for hot weather farm work.

I like the mesh crown hats for really hot weather. But these are not the best for rain, and if the temperature drops and the wind picks up, the hat can cool your head too much. I regularly wear a black or an off-white felt cowboy hat, depending on the weather conditions and what I feel like wearing. The lighter colored hat is warm, but cooler than the black one. I tried out a Buffalo Wool hat a while back, and liked it so much, I gave it to a good friend and bought another. The buffalo wool seems to breathe better than conventional wool felt, and mine can be rolled up and stuck in a pack or suitcase.

Stiff brim: The brim determines the sun protection and where the rain will drip off. If the brim is floppy—think "Beverly Hillbillies" and Jed Clampett—the water drains down the fold, wherever that might be.

Also, I theorize that a wide-brimmed hat is warmer because it slows down the heat that escapes from the collar of your shirt. This creates a warm zone that your ears will appreciate. You can try this yourself—take along a baseball cap and swap them out. I think you'll agree.

Stocking Hats

A stocking hat is also in my survival gear. A stocking hat, by way of (my) definition, is a loose knit, form-fitting cap, made of natural or synthetic fibers. The proper stocking hat can handle two vastly different scenarios.

Heat: Mississippi has got to be one of the most hot, humid places anywhere during the summer months. At least it is, as I learned, when you're wearing a wool uniform.

Flashback: One summer, I participated in Civil War reenactments as a volunteer at the Vicksburg Military Park and Old Courthouse Museum in Vicksburg, Mississippi. I dressed in authentic Civil War clothing amidst the hottest, most humid of days. We performed in living history interpretations for tourists, demonstrating aspects of the ordinary life of soldiering during the 1863 conflict at Vicksburg. Reenactors were required to be dressed as either Union or Confederate soldiers, depending on the storyline. My role in one story was to play an "unwilling conscript" who disagreed with the Confederate cause.

I protested vigorously, in the tradition of all conscripts, and pointed out the perfidy of the southern cause. At one point, I refused to stand and sing "Dixie" along with the other re-enactors. For this, and other malingering, I was tied to a cannon in front of the museum as an example to other malcontents. At one of these living history events, I noticed a soldier wearing a stocking cap, drilling in the hot Mississippi sun. He claimed it kept him cool.

"It is made of cotton, and hand-knit by my sister," he told me. "I soak it in water before we hit the field, and the evaporation keeps me cool."

For improved sun protection, he sometimes wore a broad-brimmed straw planter's hat over the wet cap. The stocking cap provided insulation from the tropical sun and a source of water for evaporation. The straw hat shaded his head, face, and neck. All his modern sun protection needs were taken care of very effectively by old-time technology.

This technique can be adapted to your desert or hot weather hiking with a cotton stocking cap. The cap will be warm at night until it gets wet. In the daytime, soak it in water to help cool your head. This cap (unless it's a beanie) can also be pulled down over your eyes, ears, nose, and neck for sun protection. A cotton bandana can also be put into service in a similar manner.

Cold: People think of thick, wool caps when they think of winter wear. I do too.

One of my favorite hunting caps is a reversible camouflage/blaze orange synthetic ski-mask. I seldom pull the cap down over my face, but I know the option is there. When big game hunting, I wear the orange side out. When after waterfowl, I use the camo. In those instances, the face covering may be used to help hide my face. A stocking cap is great to wear for stalking through deep woods, or when there is a lot of bush to go through.

My collection of stocking caps range from light to heavy. I may start out wearing a stocking cap, and then layer another on top of it if the weather or conditions call for it. Despite the versatility of stocking caps, there are a few things to consider before buying one:

- **Material:** Don't buy a cotton cap for cold weather or a wool one for heat. The material of the cap will help determine when it should be used, and you don't want to get them mixed up. Wool stays warm when wet, which makes it a bad choice for dealing with the heat.
- **Weave:** A tight-knit hat will tend to be warm, and a loose construction will allow heat to dissipate quicker. Don't get a loose weave cap for warmth.
- **Size:** A beanie is typically not large enough to cover your face and nose if needed. Conversely, a large hat may be bulky and too hot.

Naturally, you may end up in entirely different situations, and your preferences probably differ.

But a hat that protects your head should be in your survival clothing, so find one you like.

Best Wool Outdoor Pants

One of the first cold weather clothing items you should get is a pair of wool pants. If you are a bushcrafter or survivalist type who lives in the colder regions, consider the pants as an integral part of your emergency gear. Here is how to pick the right wool pants.

As always, decide where you will most likely be wearing these pants, and under what conditions. Wool may not be the best choice in hot weather, because it holds heat. But it also breathes, and that can be important for staying cool. But wool is the absolute best choice for cold, wet weather.

Conversely, there are no worse pants for winter survival than denim jeans. The cotton cloth sucks heat from your body, and once the material gets wet, the moisture wicks through the fabric until it's completely soggy.

While there are synthetic clothing options available, for my money, nothing beats wool in winter. Where I live in Central Oregon, wool is my favorite material for pants about six months out of the year.

Wool pants can be inexpensive: At the local surplus store, I purchased a lightweight pair of wool pants for $7.95. And once you find a good wool garment, it will last seemingly forever. My old Lands' End red wool sweater has served me well for the past twenty-five years, and it's still going strong. The biggest danger is my wife sending the sweater to the thrift store!

To make sure the pants will fit—be aware of "vanity sizing": On most pants, the actual waist measurement is larger than the size printed on the label. The inseam size on pants are fairly accurate, but when it comes to the waist, all bets are off. For example, I wear a size thirty-two jeans in the waist. But my actual waist size is between thirty-three and thirty-four inches. Try the pants on before buying them. Sizes vary among different brands, and American sizes are not necessarily consistent with foreign surplus sizes.

Here are some things to consider before buying any wool pants:

- **Size:** Get a couple inches or so bigger around the waist because the wool will probably shrink with use. You may want to wear polypropylene long underwear underneath, or synthetic pajama bottoms if wool makes you itch. The best choice is an under-layer of Merino wool. It will be warm, comfortable, and relatively odor free. Don't wear one hundred percent cotton thermal long johns—eventually, they will get damp from perspiration and suck the heat away. Also, you'll want plenty of room in the seat and thighs of the pants if the plans include vigorous snow sports such as snowshoeing or cross-country skiing.
- **Not too long:** While it may be the style to wear pants cuffs that drag on the ground, that isn't going to work well in snow or mud. With gaiters, you'll have to tuck the pant legs in them, and the unnecessary bulk can be a pain.
- **Lots of pockets:** I carry a BIC butane lighter in my pocket to keep the fuel warm and functioning. I also need other pocket survival gear, and having large pockets is incredibly handy. Some items, such as batteries, must be kept warm for them to function and you'll need a place to carry them.
- **Sturdy belt loops or suspender links:** Wool can get heavy, and a belt or suspenders will be needed. Suspenders are great if you don't want the bulk of a belt around your waist. They will also allow you to comfortably strap on a fanny pack or the belt of a daypack.
- **Cost:** Surplus wool pants can range in price from under ten dollars to about thirty dollars. Go to the high end Filson or L.L. Bean pants and you'll spend upward of $120. You get what you pay for, but I've never seen the need for high-priced wool pants.

The next consideration is the weight, or thickness, of the pants. Obviously, the colder the weather, the thicker the material you'll need. In the surplus arena, there are usually three different weights.

- **Lightweight dress slacks:** These are designed to go with military dress uniforms, and the fabric may be no thicker than jeans. They are much warmer than jeans, though, and are a good choice for early fall. They won't have a lot of pockets, but will be very comfortable when the weather is chilly.

- **Medium weight:** This is generally the weight I wear most of the time in the winter. They are usually standard military wear and the weight most commonly available. The medium weight are comfortable from about sixty degrees down to the teens, depending on your activity level.
- **Arctic:** I have a couple pairs of Swedish heavy-duty woolies, and they are too hot unless it is very cold. But when the temperature is in the single digits, these pants come through just fine.

Wool doesn't have to be cleaned after every use. In fact, excessive washing will eventually remove the lanolin in the fiber that makes the wool water repellent. Cleaning wool is easy. I wash my stuff after an outing with regular laundry soap and warm water, then air dry them. Initially, there will be some shrinkage but if the pants were a little large in the first place, they will soon fit fine.

Check out the local surplus or thrift stores. You might find a fine piece of wool survival gear for a very good price.

Choose the Best Socks

Cold, sore feet have a way of making you hate life. The correct boots or shoes you choose for an activity are really important, but the socks will also have a major impact.

I once chose my least-suitable boots for a cold, rainy Mississippi deer hunt. They are ordinary, uninsulated leather work shoes, not waterproof, and I chose them over my waterproof, insulated Sorels, or heavy insulated boots. The idea was to see if the right socks and felt insoles would make a difference in keeping my feet warm.

The plan was to test the comparative warmth value of several different types of socks. To do that, I had to risk cold feet. The socks were to be cotton, wool, synthetic, and a wool/synthetic blend. The consistency in this unscientific test was my tried-and-tested alpaca wool insoles.

I find these insoles used in uninsulated boots gives an extra ten degrees of warmth. This becomes particularly important when you're out in seasonal weather where it is freezing at night and warm during the day.

These types of weather conditions happen frequently when hunting elk in the Oregon high desert in the late November season. It will be really cold in the mornings when we're waiting on stands. Then, at about ten in the morning, we start moving, and the extra exertion soon makes shedding layers necessary. Those heavy, insulated boots that felt so good in the morning soon become heavy and hot.

Quality insoles and insulated socks can make all the difference when it comes to keeping your feet warm. Most of these socks are on the expensive end—we're looking at twenty to forty dollars per pair. They are an investment, so think about these factors before you put the money down for a pair:

- **Know what you are looking for.** Are the socks going to be worn in waders in cold water? In insulated boots, while you're snowshoeing or winter camping? For hiking or backpacking? All these activities might require different designs.
- **Make sure your boots aren't too small for the socks.** Sometimes, people will buy a boot that fits fine with regular socks. But the thicker, insulated socks may be too bulky. If you have to cram your feet into the boot, and they are too tight, your feet will get cold. There needs to be enough room to wiggle your toes when the boots are laced.
- **Don't buy cheap socks.** There is always the temptation to scrimp on some items, especially socks. After all, you may have a dozen pairs of cotton athletic socks to wear to the gym, so why not wear them? Get a good pair of quality insulated socks, and only wear them when the cold weather warrants it. Wear the cotton socks working in the yard or at activities where cold feet might not be an issue.

Before you start sock shopping, know how to assess warmth. Sock warmth is measured in TOGs (Thermal Overall Grade). A TOG, according to Dictionary.com, is "a unit of thermal resistance used to measure the power of insulation of a fabric, garment or quilt, etc."

A basic cotton sock, according to the Heat Holders website, has a rating of TOG 0.33. This compares to an ordinary thermal sock rating of TOG 0.89. Smartwool hunting socks have a rating of TOG 1.23. Heat Holders Socks claim a TOG rating of 2.34.

For this test, I tried out Heat Holders™ synthetics, Dachstein™ wool, and Buffalo Wool™ Trekkers. All are top-end quality socks, and all are quality products. I chose them because they represent different fibers. The cotton socks were standard Russell athletic socks, the kind bought in bundles at box stores. For this comparison, I wore a different brand of sock on each foot. Luckily, my pant legs covered up the mismatched tops!

First up were the Heat Holders and Buffalo Wool. At the end of a long, cold rainy day of deer hunting, neither of my feet grew cold. Both were comfortable to wear hiking long distances, and when I sat on a stand, they kept my feet warm.

The Heat Holders seemed to be slightly warmer than the Buffalo Wool, but they made my foot sweaty and they kept falling down. To make sure it wasn't just me, a couple of hardcore duck hunters tried out the Heat Holders to test them in waders in icy cold water.

After using the Heat Holders, both waterfowlers commented that while their feet didn't get cold, they did get sweaty. We all wondered if this could eventually lead to moisture problems in severe cold. Nobody appreciated how the Heat Holders fell down around the ankle. (I found it damned annoying.) In waders, when you're waist deep in cold water, that leads to cold feet.

One of the duck hunters ended up pulling cotton tube socks over the Heat Holders to hold them up. The Buffalo Wool are mid-calf high, and they do stay up in boots. They appear to be slightly less warm

(From left) The Heat Holders and the Buffalo Wool are thick, heavily insulated socks for winter and cold weather use. The Merino wool socks are thinner, but breathe well, and are an excellent choice for hot weather wear.

These heavy wool socks will keep your feet warm, even when wet.

than the Heat Holders, but they breathe better and my feet didn't get sweaty. They are very soft, and appear to keep their shape very well. They might be the best sock to wear over extended periods of time.

I wear wool socks year round and so do several other experienced backpackers and hikers I hang out with. I tried out the Dachstein one hundred percent wool socks and used them extensively on winter hikes and a campout in the Oregon Cascades.

To check the warmth, I wore the uninsulated shoes, and a thick cotton sock on one foot, and a Dachstein on the other and went hiking in the snow. There was no comparison in warmth. The cotton foot got cold immediately, while the wool sock kept my foot warm and toasty.

At a winter campout, I wore the same heavy Dachstein socks all day in my insulated Sorels. The temperatures were well below freezing, and the wool kept my toes warm, but by the end of the day they were noticeably damp. I switched to a dry pair, and the improvement in warmth was immediately noticeable. I always change to dry wool socks before climbing into my sleeping bag at night, and I never get cold feet while sleeping.

The Dachsteins are thick, so make sure to wear a boot that is roomy enough with them.

Any of the socks mentioned in this section might be the best choice for you. Just make sure to read the labels, find out what materials the socks are made of, and get the correct-sized boots. And remember to change your socks frequently.

Your feet will thank you.

Five Reasons to Wear Wool Socks Year Round

I wear wool socks year-round for hiking. People get it in the winter, but wool in the summer might seem a little strange.

Well, the Bedouin nomads in the Arabian and Syrian deserts have been adapting to one of the harshest climates on earth for thousands of years. They wear long, wool robes to cope with the extreme heat and cold of desert nights. According to the film *Lawrence of Arabia*, Bedouins make their own clothes from the wool of their camels, sheep, and goats. The design of the clothes is both functional and fashionable. They figured out that wool is a great material to regulate body temperature, and we can learn from them.

In my experience of learning things the hard way, what doesn't work well is hiking in one hundred percent cotton socks in water-proof or water resistant boots. Your foot perspiration will soon soak through the sock, and the boot will hold the moisture in. You'll end up walking in perpetually soggy socks that soften your feet and cause blisters. Sore feet are a given.

Wool socks come in different thicknesses and styles, and they are worth considering if you're planning a long trek, or just want to have comfortable feet on a desert hike. And wool dress socks may prove to be more comfortable in the office than any other options.

Here are five reasons why wool may be the best sock material for you:

1. **Wool insulates well:** That means the material keeps your feet warm, but will also keep your feet cooler. Your feet sweat nor-mally, and hot temperatures will just make things worse. You'll need a sock that can insulate from the ground and ambient heat as well as provide padding.

2. **Wool breathes:** Waterproof or water-resistant boots may be fine in colder weather, but they can be an abomination in hot weather. What works for me for desert day hiking is a pair of Merrell Moab Ventilators, wool socks and ankle high, breathable gaiters. Since the shoes and socks breathe, and the gaiters keep out the sand, dirt, and trail debris, this combination is comfortable, lightweight, and practical.

3. **Wool wears well:** Wool is tough. The socks I use regularly hold out well, and generally last at least a season of heavy use. Premium wool socks can last a long, long time if you take care of them, and don't wear them around the house as slippers!

4. **Wool is reasonably priced:** Heavy wool socks for winter activities are an investment, and they don't come cheap. You really get what you pay for.

   Every fall, I buy a three-pack of Merino wool crew socks at Costco, and they'll last me a season of hunting, fishing, and camping. Recycle good, used wool socks where they will be appreciated.

5. **Wool is comfortable:** Wool socks are the comfort kings. In my outdoor life, that's all I wear. In my indoor life, where I may wear a coat, slacks, and tie to work, wool dress socks are standard.

You can get cheap cotton socks at the bigger box stores for about a buck a pair, and for kicking around town, they'll probably be just fine. But it's poor logic to buy good hiking boots and then wear cotton socks in them.

And don't forget to get some thick felt insoles—they can add another ten degrees of comfort to your boots, and quality insoles may allow you to wear a lighter boot in colder weather. This is particularly nice for hunters, who may start the day sitting on a stand, and then end up doing a lot of walking. Or if you work on cold concrete all day, you may be able to wear those comfortable work boots year round.

Buy wool socks. You'll be glad you did.

Choose the Best Hiking Boots

You can't compromise quality on hiking boots. Sore, wet, cold feet can ruin an outing. In the worst case scenario, inadequate footwear could create a survival situation.

This footwear collection should cover just about any situation. (Front row, from left) Flip-flops, water shoes, low-ankle trail hikers. (Back row, from left) Ankle-high, uninsulated boots, tall, insulated hunting boots, Sorel snow boots.

Buy quality boots that fit your feet well, and make sure they are well broken-in before heading out on a hike or other adventure.

Don't do this:

Flashback: I spent the month of August, 1977, hiking in the Beartooth Mountains of Montana and Yellowstone National Park. I started out wearing a pair of Georgia brand logger boots that had seen a lot of hard use the year before.

In 1976, I wore the Georgias on backpacking trips to the Pryor and Bighorn Mountains in Wyoming. Then I wore them on the 225-mile

John Muir Trail in California, and added another twenty to thirty miles hiking across Yosemite.

The Georgias served me well, but one sole separated as we were hiking out of the Beartooths. Headed for Yellowstone in a couple of days, I couldn't find a boot repair place in Billings. So much against my better judgement, I bought a new pair of leather Lowa hiking boots to wear. Breaking in started immediately. I put them on with hiking socks, and waded in a creek outside the outdoor store to get them thoroughly soaked. Then I walked until they were dry.

A day or so later, when I was dropped off at the east entrance to Yellowstone, the boots were still stiff and inflexible. For the next fourteen days, I hiked the Thorofare Creek and South Loop. I wore the Lowas until my feet grew sore, then switched over to my Adidas running shoes. The Adidas were excellent hiking shoes on the trail. In one instance, I had to wade and hike well over a mile through a flooded meadow where beaver dams backed up the water over the trail. Without the backup running shoes, my feet would have gotten even sorer.

On my last day in Yellowstone, I walked to Old Faithful Inn in a snowstorm, wearing my soggy Adidas. The moral to the story: don't even think about breaking-in boots during a hiking trip, and take along a backup pair of shoes.

Major articles have been written about fitting boots, deciding which is best for the existing conditions, potential uses, etc. But the bottom line is always that the boots (where have you heard this before?) have to work for you.

Before investing in a pair of boots, think about what will be expected of them.

For example, you don't want insulated boots for summer treks through Southeastern swamps. But you also don't want breathable, lightweight trail runners for deep snow use. Match the shoe to the conditions. If you have questions, go to a quality outdoor store and ask. The best, all-around boot for everyone doesn't exist. But different styles and designs will most effectively match different conditions and environments.

Probably the first choice to make is: *waterproof or not?*

This waterproof low-quarter hiking shoe is great for hiking on muddy trails with a light pack.

I have both, and the conditions determine which is best. Generally speaking, waterproof are hotter and tend to make your feet sweat. If you are hiking in hot areas, your feet will sweat anyway, and with waterproof shoes, there is no way for the moisture to leave the footwear.

Yes, I've heard all the claims from the waterproof barrier folks who claim their products breathe. My experience is that just isn't so. It's all about air pressure. If the air pressure is higher outside—like when it's raining—the moisture inside can't get out.

In a low-cut shoe, the waterproofing is only good for an inch or so above the sole. This is fine if you are walking in wet grass or a muddy trail. But wading a creek in them still means you'll have to stop and empty out the water afterwards. I love waterproof boots for hunting or canoeing in cold weather. In standing water or snow, waterproof shoes will keep your feet warm and dry, even if you are wading.

As mentioned, think about where you will be using the shoe the most. Choose accordingly.

Here are the shoes/boots what work for me, based on years of hiking, wading, strolling and tromping. Check out my suggestions and improve upon them for yourself:

Barefoot: Ever since somebody on a "reality" show started going barefoot in the wilderness, hordes of imitators and emulators have come out of the woodwork. There is a barefoot hiking movement called "earthing."

As I understand it, during earthing the skin of a bare foot comes in contact with the earth, and free electrons are taken up into the body. These electrons work as antioxidants and help neutralize damaging excess free radicals that can lead to inflammation and disease in the body.

I must confess—I regularly walk barefoot around a track, when walking my dog in the summer. In Mississippi, the heat index is frequently unbearable. My reasoning is that if I can walk barefoot comfortably, my dog will not burn the pads on her feet.

Be that what it may, hiking, walking, or strolling barefoot in the wilderness is crazy.

Granted, taking off those heavy, sweaty socks and hiking boots, and walking on a cool wet, sandbar barefooted is a sensual . . . *ahhhh* . . . experience. But stub your toe, or step on a thorn, sharp rock, or piece of broken glass and you may create an *AHHHH!!!!* survival experience.

A consideration for barefoot walkers is parasites that can afflict people with no shoes. Look up "hookworm."

Flip-flops or sport sandals: Some of my personal favorites, I wear these almost constantly in warm weather. One August, my family camped on a sandy beach, next to a pine forest. Since the main recreation was water-skiing, swimming, and other water sports, footgear was minimal at best. But I noticed that nobody could walk barefoot comfortably in the woods. Pine needles, branches, and other pointy things made walking difficult.

A pair of flip-flops is light, takes up virtually no room, and shifts walking barefoot to a minimal safety level. Sport sandals can be used for hiking, but I don't like how little rocks can get trapped between your foot and the sandal sole.

Both flip-flops and sports sandals are sufficient for walking around camp, and they might keep you from cutting your foot on a pop top or piece of glass. Flip-flops are my dog-walking shoes for much of the year. I wear them while walking over sharp gravel, or when going through thick grass.

Low top running shoes: Lightweight running shoes can be fine for walking on a path. If you're going on a long hike, consider taking along a pair. You may have a boot failure at a distance from the trailhead and need to hike back.

Another nice aspect of having a light pair of shoes along is that you can switch shoes if a hot spot starts to develop on your foot. Keep a blister from starting!

Wading a stream, barefoot, with a heavy pack on your back is dangerous and foolhardy. (See barefoot section on previous page.) This is where you put on the lightweights and cross. Then tie them to the top of the backpack to allow them to dry out.

Flashback: Seeing a grizzly bear (from the safety of a vehicle or building) was on my bucket list.

On one of the innumerable stream crossings on the Thorofare Creek trail in Yellowstone, I had switched to my running shoes and waded across. There was a set of bear tracks in the sand, and a print measured as wide as my outstretched hand. The track was so fresh the water hadn't even started filling it yet.

Stumbling upon and surprising a grizzly wasn't a great idea. Singing loudly and making a lot of noise was. Nobody ever belted out "Amazing Grace" with more fervor, conviction, and volume than I did walking on that creek trail!

Low-top walking shoes: These are what I wear on an almost daily basis. I like Merrill Ventilators, and have worn out two pairs, because the color matches virtually any type of clothing. At my job at Central Oregon Community College in Bend, Oregon, my shoes matched my usual attire of dressy-casual.

Another good choice are Garmont Trekkers. These are designed for trail running and the backs of the shoe grips the heels really securely. This style of shoe is great for short hikes or walking in urban environments. If there is going to be a problem with small rocks getting in the shoes, consider gaiters.

Ankle high, uninsulated boots: For an all-around boot, this selection comes closest. My pick for this category is a pair of Danner Cougars. Mine are waterproof, and have a fairly aggressive tread. I wore these boots on Idaho and Oregon deer and elk hunts and really liked how they worked out.

When you're walking much of the day, and the temperatures range from thirty degrees at dawn to sixty to seventy degrees at noon, a heavily insulated boot is overkill. The comfort level and weight savings can be considerable. Something to consider when getting a pair of uninsulated boots is adding a quality insole. A felt insole will insulate your foot from the cold ground and can make a significant difference in overall warmth.

My choice for the closest all-around shoes are ankle high, uninsulated boots.

High top insulated boots: I've worn a pair of Cabela's Outfitters for about fifteen years, and I like them a lot. They are heavily insulated, and great for long hikes in cold weather. On frosty October mornings in the mountains, the insulation is wonderful. But in the afternoon, when temperatures have heated up into the seventies, the boots tend to feel a trifle warm. They can also feel heavy, if you're doing a lot of walking.

Still, I remember one Idaho elk hunt where it rained and sleeted constantly all day. Moving through the wet brush got me soaked. The only things dry at the end of the day were my feet!

Snow boots: Where I live in Central Oregon, a good pair of insulated boots for the cold and snow is mandatory for outdoor activities. I stick with the old reliable Sorels brand, and I have worn some variation of that product for years. But a few years back, I went to ankle-high, heavily insulated Sorels to save on weight.

My reasoning is that in deep snow, I'll wear gaiters anyway, so an additional few inches of insulated boot aren't particularly valuable.

Here are some honorable mention boot selections:

Knee-high insulated rubber boots: Sometimes referred to as "Muck" boots, these shine when worn walking through swamps with standing water. The synthetics don't carry scent, so they are a good choice for walking out to the deer stand.

On a Mississippi River canoe trip with Big River Wild Adventures, we all wear waterproof neoprene boots. The Quapaw Canoe Company guides are constantly jumping in and out of the canoes, and in cold weather that can be very uncomfortable. We don't usually wear socks in the neoprene boots, but cover our feet with Vicks Vapor Rub. This works well. At night, wiping off your feet, then walking on the sand provides another . . . *ahhh* . . . moment.

Snake Boots: If you hike a lot in southern swamps, a pair of snake-proof boots is a good idea. These boots are typically knee-high. Most snake bites occur about ankle or foot level, so you should be well-protected.

Hip waders: I wore these a lot in Mississippi when I used to hunt ducks in greentree reservoirs and backwaters. Ducks, squirrels, and deer love the standing water that ranges from a few inches to several feet deep. The hip waders will keep your feet warm and protected until you step in a hole or trip over a log!

Jungle boots: These canvas upper, military issue boots first became popular with many outdoorspeople during the Vietnam War era, and they are a good choice in many cases.

Jungle boots were my choice for a nine-day canoe trip in the northern Minnesota Boundary Waters, and they were perfect for the situation. My feet were wet constantly, but the boots offered good ankle support and an aggressive tread pattern for the daily portages over muddy trails. The jungle-style boots dry out rapidly, and are worth considering for hot, swampy scenarios.

L.L. Bean Boots: This rubber-bottom, leather-top boot is one of my favorites for hunting eastern deciduous forests, and I wore out two pairs before moving west. The design works really well in deep, damp forests, where the leaves are several inches thick.

The flexible sole is great for slipping through the woods, while providing adequate protection for your feet. I bought mine large enough so they could be worn with insulated booties or felt insoles on colder days.

Whatever boots or shoes you get, here are some add-ons that make them work better:

- **Quality insoles:** I field tested a pair of alpaca felt insoles and loved how they worked. In frigid areas, the cold seeps into your foot from below. The felt provides a cold barrier that may allow you to wear a lighter boot for comfort.
- **Gaiters:** A pair of gaiters is a great addition to any low cut shoes. They are essentially leggings that are placed over the low top shoe and they protect the ankle and shin. Gaiters weigh mere ounces, and they keep the trail trash out of your shoes. If you're hiking in an area that has cinders, sand, or volcanic scree, you will really appreciate how the gaiters keep that out. Gaiters are great in deep snow also. Rather than wear high-top snow boots, which tend to be heavy and clumsy, I'll wear a pair of ankle-high boots and knee high gaiters. If you frequent areas with venomous snakes, a pair of snake bite-proof gaiters are a sound investment.

- **Quality socks:** This topic is so important it gets its own section! Bottom line: You need quality socks to make your boots perform to their top potential.
- **Crampons:** These are spiked treads that attach to boot soles. It's easy to see their value on ice or snow, but how about in other environments?

Trust me on this: A layer of dead, wet oak leaves on saturated clay soil—like you can find in deciduous forests in the southeastern United States after a rain—are as slick as any ice. And you can fall just as hard. Crampons are also useful on your boots if you're wading a river with mossy, slick, rounded river rocks.

You might get by scrimping in some preparedness areas. But quality footwear is not one of those. Invest wisely!

Urban Camouflage: Dress Like a Grey Man

There are times when you don't want to stand out in the crowd.

You're driving home from work, something "big" just happened, and you're completely stuck in gridlock on the highway. You heard it on the car radio news—the situation is really bad, getting worse, and folks are starting to panic in some areas. The road will be blocked for hours, maybe days, and you have no choice but to start walking home.

However, you're prepared for this scenario. You abandon your car, grab your Get-Your-Ass-Home backpack out of the trunk and start walking. Columns of dazed commuters are heading for the next exit, and the off ramp dumps the crowd out in a bad part of town. The street lights are out. You're not feeling good about this at all.

How do you blend in, so you don't become a target for muggers, robbers, or worse? You want to be that nondescript person who gets ignored in a crowd.

Here are some fashion tips to get you home safely:

When I lived in Central Oregon several patterns of camo were needed, for hunting in the desert, pine forests, and deciduous forests, as well as in the waterfowl swamps. But you won't see me in camouflage when I'm in the city. Because nobody knows when the "big one" will hit.

Wearing camos during a disaster is like wearing a blaze orange sign that says, "Look at me! Look at me! I have a lot of really valuable things that you don't, including food and water!" You don't want to look like you stepped off the set of a *Mad Max* film.

The best idea in an unexpected urban disaster is to look like all the other unprepared commuters, wearing a nondescript backpack, and modestly blending in with the crowd. But your pack will be full of stuff that will help you survive and get home.

Your Get Home Bag: The stuff you need packed in your urban survival bag is another topic. Go with the kind of pack that's standard in your region. On the east coast, you might see commuter packs. In Oregon, messenger bags are popular. On any high school or college campus, backpacks are common. See what the locals use, and plan accordingly. Whatever you use, make sure it is large enough to carry everything you need, but not so large that it's too heavy to carry on a long trip.

How to Dress For Survival and Blend

Fabrics: A wool business suit is going to keep you much warmer in a wet, cold area than one made of cotton or linen. Don't buy any garment that has the potential to be worn in a survival situation without understanding the fabrics in it.

My standard outfit for teaching at the local community college helps me blend in with everyone else. I'm wearing 5.11 Taclight Pro pants, wool socks, Merrell walking shoes, and a silly tie.

Pants: Avoid one hundred percent cotton pants, like jeans or khakis unless you live in a hot climate. Cotton clothing won't stay warm for long, and the material will absorb moisture. Make good fabric choices with discreet tactical styling. Dark pants blend in easier. If you wear a long overcoat, it should cover up any pockets that might give you away as someone who is prepared.

Design: As far as I'm concerned, the more pockets in a pair of pants, the better for preparedness. My wife wishes I'd lose the pockets when we're out on the town for dinner, but I say, "That's the whole point!"

I wear tactical pants daily. I like my 5.11 Taclight Pro brand for a variety of reasons—these include the position and number of pockets, the fit, and the wear. I do wish the pants had an all-synthetic fabric, as that would be an improvement. Another good option is the 5.11 Men's Stryke for an urban survival setting. Tru Spec makes a tactical pant that looks like normal dress slacks, only with hidden pockets.

Shoes: Get sturdy, insulated, waterproof boots or walking shoes. Go with a dark color. Make sure they're broken in and nondescript. Shiny, perfect equipment may attract attention.

Flashback: I walked several blocks through several inches of slush one afternoon to catch a train in downtown Manhattan. I was wearing my L.L. Bean Maine hunting boots, a suit, a wool fedora, and a thick-lined overcoat. Many people on that street were wearing inappropriate footwear, most noticeably, a woman in a skirt and stiletto heels.

My feet were warm and dry, and I could have walked many miles in those conditions with no trouble. But many of the folks I saw on the street could not have survived a massive storm with broken down infrastructure without severe frostbite and hypothermia. They counted on the trains to arrive on time, a taxi to pick them up, enough room in a heated coffee shop for their respite, and the kindness of strangers. If one of these expected services fell down, these folks were in real trouble.

You won't be able to take a knife on board, but most of your survival gear will make it past the TSA inspectors. My backpack is drab and non-descript.

Socks: A high quality synthetic or wool sock will work. Plenty of dress socks have a nice blend in them that will also help keep your feet warm.

Underwear: I don't mind getting too personal here. Stop wearing cotton underwear. There are any number of synthetic or wool undergarments that will work better.

Shirt: Get a good synthetic blend for the climate and conditions. A one hundred percent cotton dress shirt may be your best choice if you have to walk during a heat wave. But a synthetic blend will probably be a better overall choice for any season. Long sleeves will provide some warmth and sun protection.

Tie: Whatever. Take it off and stuff it in your pack. One never knows when you'll have to tie something or someone up or down.

Overcoat: If you need a dress coat for your work, get a long trench coat in a neutral khaki color. You'll look like most of the commuters walking home. The long coat will cover your tactical black pants pockets (with your stuff), and people will only see your shins and shoes.

During the winter season, you can throw a fleece vest in the car just to prepare for the worst. I always keep clothing for layering in a bag in my car trunk to pull out if needed. Bottom line: your car should be packed with the type of coat you may need to walk miles in freezing and snowing conditions.

If you don't wear a suit to work, your standard winter waterproof jacket will do the trick. If you live in the upper Midwest, a hooded parka is completely normal and you'll look like all the other Mid-westerners in yours. Go with what the natives wear.

Gloves: Black, warm, and nondescript. I like fleece or wool gloves. They're light, warm, and comfortable. And you can layer up both when they stretch.

Hat: When I was younger and commuting to my first big city job in Washington D.C., I remember walking several blocks in the pouring rain with water dripping down my neck and soaking my shirt collar and tie. I learned my lesson. After that, I got a medium-brimmed wool hat for rainy days. It looks sort of like a businessman's hat or fedora, but has the added benefit of shedding rain and keeping my head warm. It's now my go-to hat for just about everything. In colder climates, get a wool beanie, stocking cap, or whatever you see other people wearing.

In warmer weather, and especially in the peak summer months, you want a loose weave hat to keep your head and face in the shade. At all times, have your seasonal head gear in the car with you, on your head, or at the office for the walk out.

When it comes to clothing, I wear seasonally appropriate items, (ice, snow, sun, heat, wind, rain) and I make sure my backup clothing is in the car if I need it.

A good definition of camouflage is the ability to blend in. Consider your circumstances, surroundings, and the current weather in order to plan accordingly. And change your clothing, pack, and gear with the seasons. Your goal is to get home safely, not to make a fashion statement.

Remember This:

Clothing is the first line of defense against hypothermia or hyperthermia. How effective your clothing will be depends on the fibers and materials it is made of, the insulative value, design, and fastenings. In an urban survival setting, the design and style of your clothing can either attract or deflect unwanted attention. Choose your clothing with as much care and thought as the rest of your bushcrafting gear.

CHAPTER 5
BUILDING A SHELTER

Constructing a shelter requires a lot of thought and preparation, and an emergency shelter needs to be made quickly. While the ability to construct a shelter out of natural materials is a useful survival skill, it may not be practical during a survival situation.

It takes several hours to make an efficient shelter out of natural materials. This assumes you are not injured, can gather sufficient wood, grass, reeds, etc. quickly, have the proper tools, and enough time to work on the shelter before it gets dark. And when will you decide you're lost and need to make a shelter for the night? Probably an hour or so before nightfall, right?

Here are some things to know about building a shelter.

Twelve Tips for Finding a Safe Camping Location

Flashback: The storm clouds were moving toward us, and bad weather was going to hit in a few minutes. My brother, Mike Pantenburg, and I were far back in the Idaho backcountry on an elk hunt. We had just come out of a dark, shaded drainage, and needed to find shelter quickly. We scouted the area, and set up an A-frame tarp shelter.

It rained for the next fifteen hours, but we were dry and comfortable under the tarp. Part of the reason was that we found a good, safe place to set it up. It was actually quite comfortable, and we spent the time talking and sleeping. We had been out for several days, hunting hard, and the rest was greatly appreciated.

This A-Frame tarp shelter was effective and it was quick to construct in the Idaho backcountry. It kept my brother, Mike, and me dry and comfortable for fifteen hours while it rained continuously.

Here are twelve things to look for when setting up a campsite. They are in no particular order, since the environment, topography, ground and shrub vegetation, and types of trees will play into your decisions:

1. **Wind:** Get out of the wind if at all possible. A cold wind will suck the heat out of your body and may drive rain and snow into your shelter. Look around—find the wet side of a tree and use that as a guide to show which way the wind blows in that area. Look at vegetation—in some places, it will move with the wind less, or not at all. That area is more out of the wind.

In the desert, look for large boulders, rock formations, or terrain features that break the wind, and set up your shelter in the lee side, out of the wind. Remember, a hot wind can also be dangerous because it hastens dehydration and might carry sand that will burn and chap your skin.

2. **Water drainage:** Where will storm water flow? Is there a danger of flash floods?

Flashback: It didn't seem like rain would be a problem. John Nerness, an old hiking buddy of mine, and I were in Death Valley on a backpacking trip, and the area gets about two inches of water annually. Some years, it didn't rain at all. We set up the tarp shelter in an area with rolled rocks, which indicated that at some point, water had washed through.

We were awakened by the sound of rain on the tarp. We immediately got up and moved camp to higher ground. More people die in the desert every year from drowning in flash floods than of thirst. The spot we were in probably drained a large area of land. A rainstorm a couple miles away could cause a wall of water to wash down the drainage.

Look around for rocks that look rolled, as if by a stream. In desert areas, this indicates a flash flood area. Make sure you don't choose an area that has a dip or depression that

This section of desert north of Los Angeles floods frequently. The rounded rocks show eons of high, raging water.

might cause water to pool there. The best site will be away from any known water courses, and slightly dipped to allow the water to flow away.

3. **Water access:** This is another important thing to look for. Water is heavy to carry and you will need a lot of it for drinking, cooking, and washing. The closer the water source is, the easier it will be to carry water back to camp.

    However, make sure the camp isn't too near a stream or river—a storm could cause the water to rise and flood the area.

4. **Widow makers:** In forests, the first order of business is to look up before you stop. Are there dead branches or snags that might fall in heavy wind? That's a widow (or widower) maker. Widow makers may also be rocks. If you are camped in the desert or mountain areas, there might be rocks just waiting to come crashing down. Make sure nothing will fall on you if the weather gets nasty.

5. **Snow:** In deep snow, terrain is critical, and avalanches are a real danger. An avalanche, also known as a snowslide, happens when a cohesive slab of snow resting on top of a weaker layer of snow breaks off and slides down a steep slope. Avalanche areas are

Don't build fires or set up shelters under snow-laden branches.

typically devoid of trees and other vegetation, and many have smooth snow. Don't camp on or near these areas. Watch out for snow-laden branches on trees. When it warms up, the snow will fall. You could get hit with a lot of snow that puts out fires and collapses tents and shelters. The snow could cause injuries.

6. **Game trails:** That clear area might be in the middle of a game trail, and you don't want to camp where an animal might travel at night. A cow path might be the travel route of an aggressive bull. Know what animals are in the area, and look around for poop and tracks. If you find a lot of these, move on.

7. **Warmth:** The warmest place to camp on a mountain is somewhere about halfway between top and bottom. Cold settles in the lower elevations, and higher up may be windier. Make sure your campsite is not in a cold sink, or you'll never stay warm.

8. **Drip line of trees:** Once you've decided nothing is going to fall on your shelter, consider where the drip lines of the trees will be. This is the point where moisture from rain or snow comes off a tree. When rain is the consideration, I like to place a tarp shelter about one to two feet, depending on the circumstances, under the drip line. This means the drip line will hit the top of the tarp. It is bad if the drip line is in front of the tarp—that means the rains will splash into your shelter.

9. **Sun and shade:** At noon the sun is directly overhead. Where will it be in the late afternoon? If you need protection from the sun, as in the hot desert areas, shade may be a priority. Make sure your tarp or shelter can create optimal shade.

10. **Visibility for rescue:** Assume people will be looking for you in an emergency and that you want to be found. A camp under a canopy of trees reduces the chances of being spotted from the air. Also, you will want to arrange signals for aircraft immediately, and having to clear brush and trees first will use up a lot of energy.

11. **Marshy area:** Is the proposed campsite near a swamp or standing water? These are breeding grounds for mosquitoes, and homes for snakes and other reptiles. Stay away from marshy areas unless there is no other choice.

12. **Lightning:** If you're in the mountains, don't discount the possibility of a strike. If a storm is blowing in, it may be accompanied by lightning. Don't set up a shelter under a tall, isolated tree, and consider where else might be a safe place. This could mean hunkering down among boulders or retreating downhill to a lower elevation.

If you're staying in an established campsite, you probably won't have much choice about where you camp. Let's hope the campsite was laid out with safety in mind. But if you're on your own in the wilderness, look around before you set up any camp.

Tarp Shelter Tips

Tarp shelters can make a rainy campout much more bearable. In some emergencies, a tarp might save your life.

I hiked the 225-mile John Muir trail and completed a two-week southern loop of Yellowstone using the same piece of plastic Visqueen as my only shelter. At the time, I was in my early twenties, just graduated from college, broke, and backpacking long distances. My gear choices were directly related to my financial resources!

Today, even though I have several backpacking tents, a tarp is sometimes my choice for a shelter. In some cases, such as making certain snow shelters, or when you need to go light, a tarp may be the best shelter option.

Tarp shelters are only limited by your imagination. Regardless of how you're rigging yours, here are a few proven tips I've learned that can help make your shelter more secure:

1. **Start by learning a few simple knots**, and practice tying them until you can produce an effective knot in the dark or in bad weather. Chances are, that's when you'll most desperately need a quick emergency shelter, and you don't want to be fumbling around.

    A very simple, effective shelter is the A-Frame. Basically, the A-Frame is a line set up between two anchor points, with a tarp

The timber hitch (top) secures the rope. The trucker hitch can be pulled against itself and used to tighten the line.

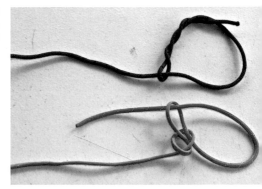

draped over it. An A-Frame looks like a pup tent without ends. These two knots will help you quickly set up a line between two anchor points.

Use a timber hitch first to secure one end of your line around a tree or rock. This friction knot is simple to tie, and the more pressure is put on the knot, the tighter it gets.

Use a trucker hitch at the other end. This hitch allows you to tighten the centerline effectively by pulling on the tag, or loose end of the cord. This hitch allows you to stretch a rope as tight as

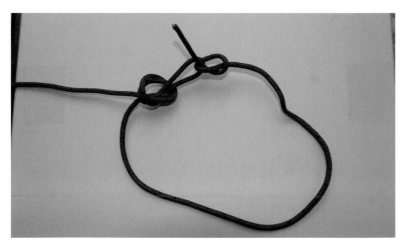

This trucker hitch allows adjustment of the tension on the main line of a tarp shelter.

a banjo string. Secure the knot by putting a couple half-hitches around it.

Drape the tarp over the taut line and weigh down the corners with rocks.

2. **Choose your campsite with an eye toward pitching a tarp.** Try to have at least one solid object to secure one end to. Always check for dead or fallen branches above and around any potential tarp site! Ideally, the ground should be slightly slanted so rain will drain easily. You may have to dig trenches around the sides to aid drainage.

3. **Insert a small stick in a rope loop in the grommet.** The concept is simple. The line is double-threaded through a grommet, and a stick is placed in the loop. This anchors the tarp at a particular point on the line, while at the same time allowing the

rope to move and be tightened. The tarp can be evenly tightened and the stick-rope combination protects the grommets from being torn in heavy winds.

During one windy, rainy campout, we used this technique (I learned it at a Peter Kummerfeldt survival seminar) to secure a

This technique allows the line to be tightened uniformly through all the tarp grommets. There is also some give, so the grommets won't be torn out as easily in heavy winds.

tarp over the cooking area and gear. The rain continued for two days, and the sticks and paracord kept the tarp taut and effective so the water drained off easily. In another instance, during a two-week campout, I left a tarp set up in this manner for fourteen days. Other than the paracord stretching some, there were no problems at all.

4. **Take along aluminum tent stakes.** They weigh hardly anything, and can be used to stake down the corners and sides of the tarp. While I typically use rocks to anchor the corner of a tarp, sometimes there aren't any handy.

5. **Don't forget your walking stick**, ski poles, or trekking poles as potential supports for a tarp shelter. In a pinch, you can use a pair of these sticks or poles to make an A-frame shelter.

6. **Keep your corner grommets from tearing out.** This tip came from my friend Bob Patterson, of Mankato, Minnesota. Bob is a retired firefighter and first responder, as well as a certified knot instructor. Knots, ropes, and lashings are his thing. Bob was also an EMT, and his job required he be out in all sorts of nasty, cold Minnesota weather. (Bob knows his foul weather gear and is my go-to guy for questions about winter camping, rain gear, or other survival clothing!) The idea here is to disperse the stress and strain, so the corner grommet doesn't get torn out by a blast of wind or prolonged gusts. Basically, you thread a piece

This setup distributes the stress between three grommets and keeps the corner from ripping out in heavy winds.

of paracord between the three grommets on a corner. The loops that result are threaded through a carabiner. With the stress dispersed between three grommets, there is not an instance when the full brunt of a gust can be focused on one grommet.

All these tips can contribute to an efficient shelter that can get you out of the nasty weather quickly. That hasty tarp shelter may be what tips the scales in favor of your survival.

How to Make a Snow Camping Tarp Shelter

A tarp shelter can provide very comfortable sleeping quarters in deep snow.

Flashback: The original plan was to build an igloo for sleeping. Eagle Scout Sean Jacox and I were at the annual Fremont District Boy Scouts Freezoree, a winter camping event in the deep snow of the Oregon Cascades. Between the two of us, Sean and I have built a couple dozen igloos, and we're very proficient at throwing up a snow shelter.

We were in about three to four feet of snow accumulation, but the snow was too dry for igloo making. The top crust went down for about a foot, then got grainy. It was like shoveling sand, and there was no way to cut blocks. So we kicked in Plan B—to make trench shelters. The directions for a trench shelter are simple: Dig a trench in the snow and cover it with a tarp.

This demonstration trench shelter was done to show how fast you could get out of the elements.

A moisture barrier, insulated pad, and effective sleeping bag made this trench shelter a comfortable place to spend a frigid night.

These shelters worked great. Though the temperatures that night got into the low single digits, both of us were very comfortable. But the shelters wouldn't have worked as well without the correct tarps, equipment, and techniques.

Here are some tips and gear for making snow trench shelters:

Get a big enough tarp: When it comes to tarps and ropes, I turn to Bob Patterson.

According to Bob, most people choose a tarp that is too small. The area around the edge is a splash/blow-in (or wet) zone, he says, that is always wet in a rain storm and even worse in a high wind. This also applies to snow and sleet.

"I have two 'go-to' tarps. Both are taffeta nylon, which is heavier than rip-stop but stronger," Patterson writes on *SurvivalCommon-Sense.com*. "One is twelve feet by twelve feet and the other is twelve feet by sixteen feet—I use the twelve feet by sixteen feet tarp the most."

In a trench shelter, you need a large enough tarp so you can shovel snow up on the edges. This becomes important if there is wind and blowing snow. Also, the size of the tarp limits the size of the trench.

Carry a good shovel: I consider a lightweight backpacking snow shovel to be an essential part of my winter Ten Essentials. Get a good one. Otherwise, that storm will blow in and you'll be forced to dig with a snowshoe or ski. That doesn't work all that well, and it isn't efficient. Another good choice, recommended by survival expert Peter Kummerfeldt, is the Snow Claw. This is a backcountry snow shovel that fits in a backpack, and works well on a variety of snow conditions. Take the tools designed for the job.

Know how to use snow anchors: Snow anchors, or dead heads, are nothing more than a stick buried in deep snow. Anchor tie a piece of rope or paracord to the tarp corner, tie a stick to that, then bury the stick in the snow. It is amazing how sturdy a snow anchor can be, and how much effort it will take to pull it out!

Cross members: Put your skis and ski poles across the trench to support the ceiling. If a lot of snow is falling, you don't want the roof to collapse. That means, you should probably also carry a saw or something to cut branches for roof supports. I like the Sven Saw. I used one in the Boundary Waters several years ago, and friends of mine in Search and Rescue include them in their gear. I've carried a folding saw in my hunting daypack for years, for processing big game animals and potential survival use.

Carry paracord: I always carry paracord, in every daypack under every circumstance. Take a minimum of fifty feet. You will use the paracord for tying down tarp ends, making "rafters" for the trench and a multitude of other things. Get the good stuff with seven individual strands.

Take along a candle: A candle can supply a surprising amount of heat in a snow shelter. At the afore-mentioned campout, I lit two in my snow trench shelter, and went off to eat dinner. When I came back in about twenty-five minutes, the candles had knocked the edge off the chill. It was still cool inside the shelter, but there was a noticeable improvement in shelter warmth. Probably more important is the morale factor. It gets dark early in the winter, and night may last fourteen hours. A candle can light the interior very well, allowing you to read or play cards. It will help you pass the time, and stay focused on surviving.

Take along a closed cell foam pad: The cold from underneath can suck the heat right out of your body. While you can rely on cutting tree boughs, and lining the floor of the trench, it's going to take a lot of extra cutting and chopping. The safest choice is to take a closed cell foam pad, because it is the least affected, and cheapest material for a sleeping pad. A quality inflatable mattress may work, but make sure you get an insulated one. I've used an Exped Downmat 7 for about fifteen years now, and it has performed magnificently. It has never leaked and helped keep me warm, even in below zero temperatures when it was the only barrier between me and the ice underneath.

Carry a space blanket: I'm talking about the sturdy, quilted blankets, with one reflector side. This will be the vapor barrier on the floor, and the reflector side will direct heat back into the pad and bag. Don't get those flimsy Mylar blankets that retail for about two dollars. They are fragile and tear easily.

Knowledge: This doesn't weigh anything, and you can take it with you anywhere. Before you go into the backcountry, anticipate a worst-case scenario, and then think about how you might deal with it. Consider what tools you need and what techniques you might need to learn.

Then practice. And prepare to enjoy yourself in the wilderness!

Ten Things to Consider Before Buying a Tent

Flashback: Some might say only a fool sleeps in a backpacking tent in July in Louisiana, but I did just that while listening to swarms of mosquitoes struggling to get past the netting. It was about ninety-five degrees, with humidity in the high nineties, and I stretched out on my sleeping bag sweating the night away, but without a single bite.

But I also recall winter camping on an Iowa night where the temperatures got to negative ten below, with a wind chill of about negative thirty. In both cases, that same tent was not particularly comfortable, but served its purpose. If you're new to bushcrafting and tent camping, you may be wondering what to look for in a tent. Here are ten things to consider:

1. **Setup:** Make sure the tent is easy to set up, and that you can do it by yourself if necessary. Practice putting it up in the backyard before going out. We've all seen people at campgrounds setting up new tents by flashlight. Not a good way to start the camping experience.

2. **Size:** Always remove one person of the allowance of people that the tent recommends. This gives you room for gear. A two-man tent, for example is just about right for me and my stuff. My wife and I fit nicely in a three-man, with plenty of room.

   Also, most state parks allow a twelve foot by twelve foot space for a tent. Anything more could overlap that allotted area. Just something to think about.

3. **Long-term or overnight camping:** If you're planning a several-day stay, such as a hunting or fishing camp, you probably want a larger, possibly heated tent. This is where a canvas wall tent comes into its own. Otherwise, a wall tent will probably be over-kill. The extra time required to set one up could get to be a pain if you're moving every day or so.

4. **Season:** Decide which season you will most likely be camping in. I prefer snow camping to any other type, so I require a four-season tent where the rain fly completely covers the tent. But a two-season is typically spring and summer, and it will be a lot lighter, cheaper, and not so warm. It will also have more mesh and ventilation for coolness. A winter tent can be miserable in summer, and vice versa.

   If the tent is going to be part of your emergency gear, think about the worst weather your area has. Chances are, that will be when you need the shelter.

These four-season tents feature a full-length rain fly. They are very comfortable for winter snow camping.

5. **Ventilation:** Manufacturers have done their best to fireproof tents by improving the fire resistance of the fabric. But what has also happened is that the material doesn't breathe anymore, and without adequate ventilation, some of these tents are like sleeping in a plastic bag. This has resulted in a lot more mesh, and more doors put in for air flow. In the winter, that air flow can be frigid. Take a look at the design, and see if the air flow is going to be a problem in colder temperatures. If it is, keep looking.

6. **Bathtub floor:** This is a floor that doesn't have long seams but wraps the bottom of the tent. If you get standing water, or water running through the camp, a well-designed floor will keep the moisture from seeping in.

7. **Backpacking:** If you anticipate backpacking, consider a lightweight, three-season tent that can take the wind well. It won't be as comfortable for a long term camp-in, but you must sacrifice some comfort for lighter weight.

8. **To stake or not:** Just about any tent has stakes of some sort. But this could become a problem if you're going to a commercial campsite with established tent pads. The ground may be so hard that staking a tent down is difficult. Many lightweight mountain tents need stakes to be set up. If you're setting up the tent on rock, this could be a real problem. Make sure to think about the possible extreme situations the tent might be used for.

9. **Wind resistance:** The taller the tent, the more kite-like it will become in high winds. More headroom equals more wind resistance. Do you like to stand up inside? Then this will require some planning. A tall center height tent may also act like a sail in heavy wind or rain. This taller tent will be cooler, which may be a good thing in the summer, but not in the colder weather.

10. **Rain fly:** The rain fly keeps the tent dry. It also regulates ventilation, and subsequently, the warmth. A four-season tent should have a fly that covers the tent completely, and effectively seals out most of the wind. A two-season car camping tent may have a partial fly and a lot of mesh for ventilation. In the summer heat, you're probably more interested in dissipating heat than in staying warm.

Buying a tent is a very personal decision. Think about what you need before investing.

How to Choose a Sleeping Bag

My canoe trip on the Mississippi River went from being uncomfortable to a survival situation in an instant.

Flashback: It was a cold, windy day on the Mississippi River somewhere around Baton Rouge. I had canoed from the river's headwaters in northern Minnesota, and was on my way to the Gulf of Mexico. The day was cold and blustery, with intermittent rain showers. My cheap, vinyl rain jacket was not keeping me warm or dry.

During a lull in the rain, I pulled off the river at a bend to change clothes and warm up. Then I walked barefoot to the top of the levee to take a look around. The idea was to build a campfire and make some hot tea. But I saw a towboat coming, so I picked my way down through the broken concrete riprap to drag the canoe up higher on the bank. As I was pulling on the canoe near the back, my foot hit the slippery moss on the rocks and I landed inelegantly in the river. By the time I got out of the frigid water, some one hundred yards downstream, my body was thoroughly chilled.

Long story short: my sleeping bag probably saved my life. I was able to get back to the canoe, strip off my wet clothes, and warm up in the sleeping bag.

One piece of gear you don't want to have to improvise is a sleeping bag. If you can't sleep at night because you're cold, the next day is guaranteed to be exhausting.

And hypothermia can be a very real threat, even if the ambient temperature feels warm. But you don't want just any sleeping bag, and you need one that is adapted to the circumstances or environment you might encounter.

I slept on top of a sleeping bag in Louisiana one night in July, when the nighttime temperature was about ninety degrees. I snuggled deep in an arctic bag one night during a raging Iowa blizzard when the temperature got to negative ten degrees, not counting wind chill. Today, I have close to a dozen sleeping bags, ranging from indoor sleepover styles to a pair of negative fifteen degree winter bags. All have their specific purposes. You will decide what the best sleeping bag is for your needs.

Here are some considerations to help you decide which sleeping bag(s) to get:

Where the bag will be used: Location is important. If you will be tent camping, you won't need as warm a bag as if you're sleeping under the stars. But that doesn't mean you can or should buy a cheap, light bag! If you are anticipating an urban survival situation where the power might be out in the winter, a cheaper, less durable bag may suffice. But if the bag may be packed into the backcountry, get a sturdy, heavy duty style.

Possible uses: The size, weight, and composition of the insulation will all be determined by the potential uses of the bag. A backpacking mummy bag is different than a full-cut bag designed for car camping. The car camping or elk camp sleeping bag that won't be carried anywhere can be roomier, bigger, and heavier. If you intend to backpack or canoe, you'll need something smaller and more compact.

Mummy or full cut: These are the two main styles of bag. You wear a mummy bag, so if claustrophobia is an issue for you, don't get one! (One of my mummy bags is so snug-fitting it feels like I'm wearing a loose sausage casing. It doesn't bother me, but make sure to crawl inside any prospective bag in the store before buying it.) A full-cut bag is roomier, but the additional bulk and weight makes it less ideal for backpacking.

Type of insulation: Sleeping bag insulation can be broken down basically into two categories: down and synthetic. Decide before buying: What is the potential for the bag getting wet? Goose down insulation is the classic insulation used in sleeping bags and despite all the technological advances, is still the most efficient insulation around. Goose down provides the most warmth for the least bulk

This synthetic-insulated sleeping bag will air out and dry quickly in the sun. A down bag, while lighter, may take a lot longer to dry.

and weight, allowing for very warm sleeping bags that are in very, very small packages.

But goose down insulation is *useless* when wet, and it can take forever to dry. This could be deadly: What if you fall in a creek, soak all your gear and desperately need to warm up? Or suppose part of the bag absorbs water inadvertently during a rain?

My first synthetic bag was carefully chosen. Starting out in 1976, I didn't have any gear, and accumulated it as my budget permitted. My sleeping bag was bought at an upper end backpacking store for about eighty dollars, which at the time was about a third of all my "assets." (Point of reference: in 1976, I made $1.70 per hour, working at a Hy-Vee grocery store in Ames, Iowa.)

The summer of 1976, I decided to go backpacking in the mountains. Trips to the Bighorn and Pryor Mountains in Wyoming only whetted my appetite for more, and I couch-surfed at John Nerness's house in Mountainview, California between trips. In addition to several weekenders around Central California, my grand finale was a 225-mile, fourteen-day hike of the John Muir Trail in the Sierras.

That same synthetic bag served me well on all those treks. It also was my only sleeping bag on my end-to-end Mississippi River canoe trip. Today, I don't own a down bag. But I must admit, the tiny, light bundles the down bags compress into are very appealing!

Synthetics: There are a variety of good synthetic insulation fills on the market, and generally you'll get what you pay for. Check the Internet and manufacturers' specifications to decide which will be best for you.

My first synthetic bag paid for itself in my first two days in the Sierras. Here's an excerpt from my 1976 John Muir Trail Journal:

Sunday July 25
"Last night was the worst I've spent in the mountains so far. It rained all night, and I got completely soaked in my sleeping bag. The rain started after I was sound asleep, and drenched me before I even woke up. (I'd slept under the stars, and not bothered to set up the tarp.)

The bag kept me warm, but it sure was wet and clammy. Stayed awake most of the night. The rain kept stopping, then pouring down, so I kept getting wet, then getting wetter.

My camp was at 10,500 feet, so the temperature was pretty cold. Some of my clothes got wet, but I made sure to keep my boots dry.

Got up, wrung out the sleeping bag and placed everything on rocks to dry. The sun is just coming up over the mountains, and the sky is clear. Looks like another nice day."

It rained intermittently for nine days straight after that and keeping anything dry was a real struggle. I'm glad I didn't have a down bag on that trip!

Weight: Sleeping bag weight is supposed to be a determination of how warm the bag might be. But beware! A lightweight down sleeping bag will be very warm, while a heavy, cheap cotton-filled bag will be heavy and cool. A better indication of warmth is probably the temperature rating.

Temperature Rating: My experience is that the manufacturers are very optimistic and that these ratings are more a statement of purpose than anything else! My personal rule of thumb is to look at the temperature rating and subtract twenty degrees.

Also, some people sleep colder than others. My snow camping equipment consists of a four-season dome tent and a minus fifteen-degree sleeping bag. I have slept comfortably in that setup in below zero temperatures, during blizzards with gale-force winds. But my wife took the same gear on a June Girl Scout camp-out in Oregon and was very comfortable. What about getting sleeping bags that zip together so the loved ones can snuggle? Again, this will depend on the couple. If one is a colder sleeper than the other, both will be miserable.

Make your sleeping bag choices wisely. Otherwise, you may have some really long, uncomfortable nights to ponder and regret your hasty choices!

Remember This:

A practical shelter can be the deciding factor in your survival outdoors overnight. It is very difficult to make one out of natural materials, even if you have the correct building materials, tools, skill, and time. A better choice is to always carry shelter-making materials, which can include a large plastic bag, a tarp, or lightweight backpacking tent.

A quick, efficient shelter, or better yet a quality sleeping bag and tent, can take all the dread out of an unexpected night out.

CHAPTER 6
SELECTING SURVIVAL TOOLS

The use of tools is one thing that separates humans from animals. The ability to use tools has been a crucial part of human evolution.

When it comes to bushcrafting, the right tools are literal lifesavers. These tools allow the user to build shelters, process firewood, gather food, and create other tools and containers. Therefore, you should choose your bushcrafting tools carefully.

Ten Things to Look for in a Bushcraft/Survival Knife

You can't come up with a more popular bushcraft debate topic than knives. The best "this" or "that" knife is the subject for endless discussion around campfires, in hunting camps or online. While many of us may know what we *don't* want in a knife, a better topic might be *what things do you look for?*

Let's start by deciding what we're talking about.

In this case, we're considering that mythical, all-around, "If you could only have one" knife that would be able to do everything.

It should be a good bushcraft knife. You may be whittling sticks, cleaning fish, processing tinder, stripping bark, etc., for long periods of time. The knife must also be able to handle survival tasks, such as field dressing deer or other big game animals, building shelters, cutting rope, and whatever else comes along. In the worst case scenario, the knife would have to be an effective weapon.

This perfect, jack-of-all-trades knife doesn't exist. What works for me might be a bad choice for you. The best advice might be to consider possible survival scenarios, what tasks might arise from it and what knife would work best. The other thing to consider is knife laws in your area. Find one that complies with local regulations or face possible legal complications.

Everyone has different ideas about what they need in a survival/bushcraft knife. Here are my preferences:

1. **Folder or rigid blade?** I carry folding pocket knives daily. There is a Swiss Army Classic knife on my keychain, and it gets used virtually every day. For going on fifteen years, I've carried the same Swiss Army Knife Tinker in a belt sheath. The Tinker has two blades, a can and bottle opener, toothpick, tweezers, and a Phillips screwdriver. This knife costs under twenty dollars and if I lose it, there probably won't be major emotional trauma.

    A Buck model 671 folding hunting knife rode on my hip on my 1980 end-to-end Mississippi River voyage and it did everything I needed a knife for. Later, I used that same Buck to field dress my first deer. To date, that knife has processed thousands of fish and many small game animals.

    But I won't carry a folder as a bushcraft or survival knife. The weak point of any folder is the hinge. Break that, and you end up with two pieces. As a cooking knife, the folder's hinge and blade slot can get all sorts of disgusting stuff in it that you don't want in your food.

    So, my bushcraft knife would have a rigid blade knife, but it may not be the best choice for all situations.

    In an urban environment, discretion is the best idea. A folder with a decent-sized three-to-four-inch blade can be more easily concealed than a rigid blade knife. And, a nondescript-looking, slipjoint pocket knife may be a lot less threatening-looking than a rigid blade. A slipjoint, which doesn't have a lock to hold open the blade, is also legal in some areas where a lock blade is not.

(From left) My belt knife has a three-to four-inch blade. The one I carry the most is this Kellam Hawk with a three-inch blade. The Swiss Army Tinker rides in a belt sheath. A Swiss Army Knife Classic is an incredibly useful little knife and it is attached to my keychain.

2. **Steel:** At some point, the blade will need sharpening, and you must be able to do it easily. There are many fine carbon steels and they are usually easier to sharpen than many stainless varieties. The downside is that carbon steel can rust in humid climates, and over time, they will build up a patina.

    My preferences in blade steels runs toward 1075 and 1095 carbon steel, CPM 3V and A2. A reputable knife maker must use good steel, and if a company has been in business for a while, that's a pretty good indication that their knife components are good.

3. **Full tang:** This refers to a blade that runs completely through the handle. This is the strongest option and what I prefer.

4. **Blade length:** A blade between four to six inches works for me. Now, it is possible that you've field-dressed all sorts of big game with your pocket knife! Sure it can be done—legendary outdoors writer Jack O'Connor killed many, many species of big game, all over the world. He used a basic pocket knife for most of his big game field work. But for a big game hunting knife, a

four-inch blade is all you need. I prefer about a five-inch blade in an overall knife.

5. **Blade thickness:** Many professional butcher knives have relatively thin blades, because their purpose is to slice effectively. I like about a ⅛-inch blade thickness or less. For me, that thickness is the best compromise, and it will slice, whittle, and cut, without being so thick as to be ineffective.

   For a fillet or boning knife, you want a thin blade with some flexibility. For a hunting knife, a sturdy blade that can take the hard twisting and cutting of field dressing a large animal is a good choice.

6. **Spine:** The side of the blade opposite the edge is the spine. It is frequently ignored, but it can be a useful part of the knife. I want the spine to be ground like an ice skate, with ninety-degree angles. This spine allows the user to scrape a ferrocerium rod to make sparks, shave pitchwood for tinder, and other tasks that preserve the edge of the knife.

7. **Handle:** A frequently overlooked design feature is the handle. In a survival or bushcraft knife, you may need to use the knife for long periods of time to process tinder, carve wood, make shelters, etc. How well the handle fits your hand is more important than what it is made of in these situations.

A knife handle should fit your hand. The design will determine how well it works for you.

The last time I cut myself with a knife was due to a handle failure combined with stupidity on my part. I was using a name brand bread slicing knife with a slender, skinny handle. It fits my wife's smaller hand perfectly, but the handle doesn't work for me. Anyway, I was slicing bread, my daughter was headed out the door, and I was attempting to make dinner plans with the back of her head. Amidst my inattentiveness, the slim handle twisted in my hand and sliced the tip of my finger.

Choose the handle of your knife by physically trying it out if possible. If you order a knife from a reputable company, they will allow you to exchange it if everything is not acceptable. Don't put up with a handle that doesn't feel right.

These three different knife points have different uses and configurations. (From top) They are clip, spear, and drop points.

8. **Sheath:** A well-designed sheath secures the blade and keeps it from being dangerous while not in use. The sheath should be convenient to carry and comfortable to wear on your belt. In an emergency situation, you may end up wearing your knife all the time, and it must ride comfortably.

9. **Point design:** This is another aspect that you'll have to decide. I narrow point design down to drop, clip, and spear designs. Any of these will work well for a bushcraft or survival knife. The drop point is my favorite for an overall knife, but I also really like clip points, mostly because of the looks and how well they work on hunting blades.
Briefly, here is the difference:

- **Clip:** The clip is really a variation of the drop point, and is generally associated with Bowie knives. The first knife I bought had a six-inch clip point blade. I was about thirteen at the time, and from my reading, and various TV shows, had determined that a clip point would be the best choice for hunting in Iowa. Come to find out, the blade was way too big for processing small game animals, and I ended up using my Stockman model pocket knife for just about everything. But I used a Buck model 671 folding hunter with a clip point while deer hunting for years. It has the right combination of upswept point for gutting, and enough belly on the blade to be a good skinning knife. When I replaced my trusty Buck with a survival knife, I purchased a Cold Steel SRK with a clip point.
- **Spear:** This point is right in the middle of the blade, hence the name. It is a very common point on broadswords or stabbing weapons, but is also useful for a bushcrafting knife. There is enough belly to make it a passable skinner, and the point is another good all-around choice. As a weapon point, this might be the best option. It makes a good choice for thrusting and slashing, and in general, anything you'd need a fighting knife for. My Boy Scout knife, and the legendary Kephart pattern bushcraft knife, have spear points, and they are good all-around cutlery choices.
- **Drop point:** The back, or unsharpened spine, runs straight from the handle to the tip of the knife in a slow curve, which creates a lowered point. This lowered, or drop, point provides more control and adds strength to the tip. The tip on a drop point won't be as sharp as a clip point, but it will be stronger. This tip strength

makes drop point blades popular on tactical and hard use survival knives.

10. **Blade grind:** I don't want serrations or any other specialty grind. For a do-it-all, choose between a convex, Scandi, or flat grind. Any of these will serve you well:

- **Convex:** The bevel on each side of the blade is slightly rounded as they taper to form the edge.
- **Scandi:** A short, flat, or hollow grind on a thin blade where the primary grind is also the edge bevel.
- **Flat:** A flat grind begins at the blade's spine and tapers down to the edge.

In the case of a dedicated bushcraft knife, the Scandi grind might emerge as the winner. The grind creates a good wedge, which works well for splitting wood. It's also easy to sharpen.

But most of my favorite user survival and hunting knives have a convex grind. I find the convex stays sharper longer, and makes a better skinning knife. Either a convex or Scandi will work fine.

That was ten things to look for. Here are two bonus aspects:

1. **Warranty:** The only warranty I'm interested in is the unconditional, lifetime type. A manufacturer can't afford to replace a lot of knives regularly, and a lifetime warranty shows credibility. I like knowing there is a no-hassle clause in my investment.
2. **Not tactical looking:** The fast-opening, black-colored "tacticool" combat knives don't do much for me. And a knife designed primarily for fighting probably won't be the best all-around user knife.

In knives that might be used in city settings, go for urban camouflage when possible. I got my daughter a Benchmade Griptillian folder with pink grips and my son a Griptillian in orange. Both knives look cute and harmless, but are solid, dependable tools.

I also don't like blade coatings. While they might provide some protection from rust, complete rust protection comes from maintaining the blade. Coating makes the blade drag and inhibits the slicing ability. Eventually, the coating will wear off anyway.

So, in the final analysis, for a do-it-all survival/bushcraft knife my needs will best be met with a four-inch, ⅛-inch thick, Scandi or convex grind rigid blade, drop point knife. It must be full tang, with a well-designed handle. The knife will come with a safe, well-designed sheath that is comfortable to carry. It will be unconditionally guaranteed, and preferably made in America.

This type of knife works for me and has for decades. Hopefully, you can use my choices as a place to start your own shopping.

Hatchet or Saw?

We'll assume you already have the bushcraft knife and basic Ten Essentials, and are assembling the rest of the tools needed for a portable survival kit. Do you need to add a hatchet or a small saw?

It depends. Some might call this collection a "Bug Out Bag," or something along those lines. This kit will have to cover a wide range of situations.

Saws and hatchets each have advantages and disadvantages. When choosing any bushcrafting tool for wilderness or urban survival, start by anticipating where the tool might be needed and what tasks it must perform.

Could you end up in a cold wilderness environment, where gathering firewood to keep a campfire going will be critical? Will the tool be mostly carried, or do you anticipate remaining somewhat sedentary and that the tool may be used a great deal? Will you need to saw or hack bones to butcher large animals?

Or might the tool be used in an urban setting, where the primary uses might include breaking up pallets and splitting wood scraps from a dumpster for firewood? In an extreme situation, might this tool need to be used to break down a door, gain forced entry into or egress from, a locked vehicle? In a really extreme situation could this tool be an effective weapon?

Basically, your choice for wood processing is going to boil down to two: hatchet or saw? Circumstances will most likely determine which is best for you. Here is how to decide:

Hatchet

A hatchet is a small axe that can be wielded with one hand, and the flat part may be used as a hammer. A hatchet is a great tool for splitting wood, limbing trees, and hammering in tent stakes.

Many settlers on the American frontier had a large axe as their primary tool. The axe may have been the only tool available for making a log cabin, splitting rails for a fence, and cutting firewood. Essentially, the axe only had two parts: the head and the haft, or handle. If the handle broke, it was possible to carve another out of a piece of hickory or some other hardwood.

A hatchet can be sharpened with a flat rock. This means that for long-term survival, the hatchet can be a tool with incredible durability.

The downside to a hatchet is that it can be extremely dangerous in untrained hands. Axes and hatchets cut with velocity, meaning the tool has to be swung with considerable force to chop anything. One of these tools can cause serious injury if it ricochets off

(From top) The crash ax is a tactical tool, designed to be carried by a first responder. The half hatchet can also be a hammer. The last hatchet is a standard hardware store hatchet.

the wood or other hard surfaces. Today, few people ever develop the necessary eye-hand coordination to accurately use a hatchet.

During my days working on construction crews, it was not unusual to swing a hammer all day, either framing or setting steel pans to pour concrete foundations. (My first job out of college, with my brand new journalism degree, required a wardrobe with a hard-hat, steel-toed boots, and insulated coveralls. My basic tools started with a 22-ounce framing hammer and 25-foot steel tape. I still have the hammer.) Subsequently, all this hammering and pounding developed my eye-hand coordination to a high degree. With this transferable skill, I can safely use a hatchet. But physical skills are perishable, so I never take for granted my hammering and chopping abilities.

There are many different types of hatchets for different jobs. Among my hatchet collection is a modern Estwing double-bitted, a Plumb carpenter's axe, an Estwing Sportsman, a Huron Half Hatchet, and a custom, handmade pipe tomahawk that matches my flintlock rifle. I also have several full-sized axes that are used in camp.

Here are three hatchet types the bushcrafter could consider:

1. **Crash ax:** A crash ax is not designed to be a chopper or wood-splitter, even though it performs those tasks well. The crash ax has a tactical design and is meant to be carried by a first responder who might need to hack down a door or make a quick entry into a wrecked car.

    There is a difference between tactical and traditional, wood-cutting hatchets. A woodcutting hatchet is a tool that will be used repeatedly, and it probably has softer steel so that it doesn't chip when it hits a knot or hard spot. That means the edge will roll when it hits an obstruction, but that it will require sharpening more often.

    A tactical hatchet is a tool that will be carried and (probably) rarely used. But it needs a tougher steel that can withstand hacking into all sorts of materials. It must also have a design that makes it a better weapon. The spike opposite the edge in the crash ax would be very useful for breaking car safety glass and as a weapon.

2. **Half head:** This style is so named because it has a hatchet head opposite a hammer head. This makes for a very versatile tool that can chop and pound. You'll find the hammer head is used a lot for pounding in tent stakes and such tasks around camp.

3. **Utility hatchet:** This is a tool box standard that may be called upon to do a variety of tasks. This is typically the least expensive hatchet, and one is available in any hardware store. Mine weighs about one pound.

The last hatchet I will mention is a tomahawk and I carry it for fun.

My buddy, the late Jim Grenfell, was fascinated with ancient weapons. When he heard I hunt with a flintlock .40 caliber Pennsylvania rifle, he claimed I only had part of the kit. The tradition, Jim said, was that after finishing making a rifle, the gunsmith would take the leftover chunk of wood from the rifle stock blank, and a piece of gun barrel, and fashion a matching tomahawk. No Long Hunter, he pointed out, would be caught dead without his tomahawk, because if the rifle didn't fire, the 'hawk was his backup!

So Jim made me a pipe tomahawk that matched my rifle. I still carry the tomahawk, along with the powder horn, shot bag and other accouterments when I hunt with a black powder firearm. The tomahawk could be used to help quarter a deer or field dress small game.

But I mostly take it along because the tomahawk looks so cool tucked in the back of my sash next to the powder horn! When I take a break in the field, it's enjoyable to stick the tomahawk in a tree, lean the long rifle up against it, and hang the powder horn and shot bag off the rifle barrel. Then, I sit and admire the workmanship of my tools while chewing on jerky and hardtack.

Saw

Despite my enjoyment of tomahawks and history-related weapons, I usually carry a saw in my daypack. As a big game hunter, I need a tool that can work through the pelvis of a deer, hog, antelope, or elk. Sometimes you need a saw to cut through the ribcage of a big elk. And while I can disjoint the lower legs of an elk or deer with a good hunting knife, the saw is quicker.

If you're saving horns or antlers, a saw is almost mandatory. I haven't seen anyone use an ax or hatchet to chop the antlers off anything, but I did loan my Pac-Saw to a guide once so he could take the antlers off a moose skull.

Wilderness survival expert Peter Kummerfeldt is a proponent of carrying a saw instead of an axe. He carries a seventeen-inch, double edged saw made by Dandy.

"You can give your saw to someone to gather wood, and they probably won't hurt themselves," he said. "But with a hatchet, an inexperienced user could severely injure himself."

I have several folding saws I regularly use, and generally have a couple along. My Swiss Army knife has a very usable, small saw blade, and so does my Leatherman Wave. Both saw blades work well for sawing through a deer pelvis bone, removing lower legs for quartering, and either blade will easily saw through a stick the size of my wrist.

For hunting, I carry a double-edged, single piece Pac-Saw with both wood and bone teeth. I also used a Sven Saw, a fold-up wood

These represent several different styles of saws. (From left) A take-down bow saw, folding limbing saw, Leatherman saw, Pac-Saw, and wood saw with push blade.

saw, during a ten-day canoe trip in the Boundary Waters of northern Minnesota. It proved to be an effective and lightweight tool.

As I see it, the primary reasons for including a hatchet and/or saw in your survival kit are to gather firewood and build shelters. It takes an incredible amount of firewood to keep a campfire burning throughout the night, and the person with a survival mindset will start gathering wood as soon as possible. In a pinch, it is safe and effective to pass out your saws and have everyone start gathering wood.

So which tool do you want to include in your gear? As usual, it will depend on your skill level, potential needs, and willingness to practice.

Water Purification

As a newspaper reporter covering various natural disasters, including tornadoes, floods, and forest fires, I noticed a common aspect among them. Drinking water was always in short supply. My first flood taught me that.

Flashback: I was working for the *Vicksburg Evening Post* and was sent to photograph the high water in Chickasaw Bayou, north of Vicksburg, Mississippi. The nearby Mississippi River had reclaimed some of its flood plain, sending high water into a subdivision and forcing residents to leave. I rode in a jon boat with a sheriff's deputy, and we cruised the flooded streets looking for people who might need help. It was Mississippi summer hot and the heat reflected off the muddy, nasty water and the bottom of the metal boat. We baked in the sunshine. There were miles and miles of water, but not one drop to drink (to update and steal a cliché from "The Rime of the Ancient Mariner"). I would have grown very thirsty, except the deputy was prepared with extra water and willing to share.

The other end of the spectrum was in Death Valley, California. My hiking partner, John Nerness, and I were doing a three-day backpacking trip. There was a spring on the map, but we never planned

This stock tank has plenty of water, but it must be purified before drinking.

This water hole was filled after a rain. The water won't last long and it will need to be purified.

to rely on it. The three gallons of water we each needed to carry weighed twenty-four pounds. The terrain was extremely arid and we didn't find any water anywhere.

Later, in the Oregon backcountry, I came across a desert spring. The local livestock and wildlife had dug up and muddied what little water was seeping out of the ground and pooped all over. It made a hog wallow look clean. Making that water fit to drink would have been quite a job.

Wherever you are, you need safe drinking water. There is no substitute, and soft drinks or the so-called energy drinks may not keep you hydrated. In fact, some of these soft drinks are diuretics, which will speed the removal of moisture from your body.

But water alone is not enough to keep a person hydrated. Electrolyte-enhanced waters have things like potassium and sodium added to them, which help your body absorb the water more quickly. These electrolytes are helpful in preventing dehydration, so they're especially useful during and after intense workouts or working in the heat.

How much water do you need? The general rule of thumb is to store one gallon of water per person per day, according to the Centers for Disease Control and Prevention, just for drinking. They also suggest that, in an emergency situation, you should drink a minimum of two quarts (half a gallon) of water a day—more if you're in a hot climate, sick, pregnant, or a child.

This is all well and good for the most basic drinking needs, but hardly adequate for daily needs. For washing, laundry, cooking, etc. you will need much more. Storing water is a great idea. But if you're out in the wilderness or bushcrafting, you need to be able to purify whatever water you might find.

My home in Central Oregon is within striking distance of high desert, mountains, temperate rain forests, the Pacific coast and beautiful deciduous forests. I love to roam all these areas, and frequently end up miles from the vehicle and my backup water supply. But these areas all require different variations of hydration gear. Here's how to decide what will work best for your region.

One important consideration before choosing hydration gear is to understand how long it will take to work. Some sport bottles with water filters work instantaneously—you fill them up, prime the filter, and drink. This is invaluable if you need to quickly rehydrate a child, or someone who is dehydrated to the point of medical emergency.

The best solution for hydration is to carry a variety of methods. My preference for a quick filter solution is the Nalgene Filter System. The bottle holds thirty-two ounces and it draws relatively easily and immediately. The LifeStraw is also an immediate filtration solution that allows you to draw water from any source for immediate drinking.

The chemical treatments, such as the Polar Pure, can require upward of thirty minutes to work, depending on the water temperature. Generally speaking, boiling is not a particularly quick operation. The time it takes to boil water varies, depending on altitude,

These are the three container styles I rely on. (From left) The Nalgene military style quart bottle takes up less space and doesn't roll around. The thirty-two-ounce Nalgene wide mouth has a really good filter system that can be added to it. The Platypus collapsibles take up hardly any room, weigh next to nothing, and can be filled in the field.

heat source, shape of container, etc. Then the water will have to cool down enough to drink.

You must have durable, large capacity water containers available. If you're out all day in the desert or a flood, for example, there probably won't be a place or chance to replenish your drinking water, and all you'll have is what you carry. Also, you might find someone without any water at all.

Here's what I carry as part of my hydration system, and so far, everything has served me well. (Many of these items are multi-use):

- **Nalgene bottle:** I like the wide-mouth model and modify mine with a paracord loop and duct tape. The loop is designed so the bottle can be carried on my belt or tied to a cord to lower into a stock tank, depression, or water source that is hard to get to. Don't think you can just tie something onto the lid retainer—chances are it will break at some point, and as these things go, probably when you need it the most. Nalgene also has a water filter that fits right inside the standard thirty-two-ounce wide mouth bottle. The filters are lightweight, compact, and relatively easy to drink from. I also wrap several feet of duct tape and some paracord around my bottle. These items are useful for everything, and the water bottle is a convenient place to carry them!
- **Platypus flexible water containers:** These collapsible water containers are available in various sizes as water storage units and they roll up into a small, lightweight pack when empty. I generally carry a couple large-sized extras, rolled up and empty, in my daypack, since they weigh next to nothing and don't take up much space. Then, if you need to carry water from a spring or other water source, you won't have to improvise. (Tip: since you will probably need a minimum of a gallon of water per day, it makes sense to take enough flexible water containers to haul a gallon!)
- **Tin or metal cup:** This is for boiling or dipping water out of hard-to-reach places. Boiling water may prove to be the safest, most effective method of water purification available, providing you have a heat source. A tin cup works great and is incredibly

useful. How long should you boil the water to purify it? Bring the water to a boil, and that should kill anything that boiling will kill. Water boils at 212 degrees Fahrenheit, then vaporizes. Extended boiling will not make the water hotter or kill more nasties, but it will use up more of your fuel! I usually carry a large (about twenty-four-ounce capacity), metal cup for several tasks. My large blue enamel cup and a spoon comprised my mess kit for a nine-day canoe trip in the Boundary Waters in northern Minnesota. I never needed anything else. I have brewed countless cups of tea or coffee over various heat sources with that piece of gear, and I don't leave home without one!

- **Polar Pure or Potable Agua:** These are chemical purifiers, and require a certain time period for them to work. I used the Polar Pure system exclusively on a nine-day canoe trip in Minnesota's Boundary Waters and the system worked really well. Potable Agua comes in capsules or packets and is easy to carry and use. Either Polar Pure or Potable Aqua goes on every outing.
- **Six-foot piece of aquarium tubing:** I got this tip from Peter Kummerfeldt. Peter recommends including the tubing in case you find water in a crack or crevice and can't get to it. Just stick the tube in the water and suck it out.
- **Coffee filter and bandanna:** If you can filter the mud and debris out of the water, it will make any filter last that much longer. In especially turbid, muddy water, wrap the coffee filter around the bottom of any filter and attach it with a rubber band. The bandanna has many uses, including serving as a water filter. A clean one that you haven't used to wipe your nose is preferable!
- **Large garbage bag:** Another multi-use item. Use this to catch rain or dew, or as a reservoir for holding water.
- **Water filter:** Some lightweight method of filtering and purifying water can be incredibly useful. Several companies make sport bottles with filters in them. Using them is simple—fill the bottle and suck the water through the filter. These are the best for hikes along streams, or in areas where you know there is running water

available. If the water is really nasty, two drops of plain chlorinated bleach or iodine can be added to each refill before filtering. This will kill minute pathogens such as viruses, and the disinfectant will then be filtered from the water entirely, removing its odor, color, and taste.

Include a variety of water purification solutions in your urban or back country survival kits. (From left) Polar Pure, LifeStraw, and Nalgene bottle with filter system.

So, these items work for me. My hydration system is set up with the premise that there is a piece of equipment along that *should* be able to handle any situation. Do your research, select your equipment carefully, and include an integrated hydration system in every survival kit.

And stay hydrated in the first place!

How to Choose a Magnetic Compass

Flashback: My Globe Positioning System was acting weird. I was in the high desert west of Bend, Oregon and knew the area. My compass said I was right on course. The coordinates on the topographic map agreed. But the GPS claimed the parking lot was about half a mile when I could see my car about fifty yards away.

In another instance, my brother, Michael Pantenburg, was following an elk trail down into a steep Idaho ravine. When he checked his GPS, there was no connection to the satellites. He navigated out of the area with his compass.

Magnetic compasses are sometimes taken for granted, or ignored, in favor of a GPS. But any GPS is only as reliable as the batteries in it. Or, you may find yourself in an area where the GPS can't connect with satellites.

Here is a good rule: Don't go anywhere off the pavement without a quality magnetic compass and know how to use it. But there are a

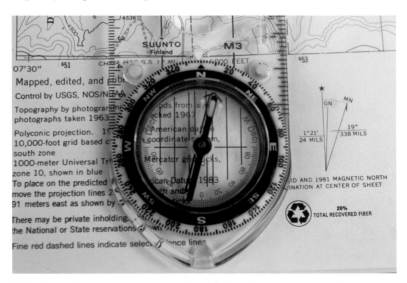

This baseplate compass is set for declination, has map scale information, and a small magnifying glass.

bewildering array of compasses on the market, and they come in all sorts of configurations. How will you pick the best compass for your particular requirements?

I asked navigation expert Blake Miller what he would recommend. Blake Miller has made a career out of staying found. His formal navigation training began when he joined the US Navy in 1973. He served as a navigator on several Navy ships over his twenty-year career. Blake began working with satellite navigation systems at sea in 1976, culminating with the then-new Global Positioning Systems aboard the Battleship *Wisconsin*. As a volunteer, Blake teaches navigation and survival classes, to students in the local school district and conservation groups. He is a member of a Search and Rescue team.

Blake suggests a good baseplate compass for outdoor travel. Key features include:

- **Declination adjustable** as I don't recommend a compass that can't be adjusted for declination. The packaging will state "declination adjustable." Some cheap compass packaging states that the compass has declination scales; this is not the same thing. Declination is a magnetic variation that must be adjusted for with the compass. "At most places on the Earth's surface, the compass doesn't point exactly toward geographic north. The deviation of the compass from true north is an angle called "declination" (or "magnetic declination"). It is a quantity that has been a nuisance to navigators for centuries, especially since it varies with both geographic location and time, according to the United States Geological Survey.
- **Liquid filled housing** to dampen the magnetic needle
- **Two degree increments** on the bearing dial of the compass housing.
- **A clear baseplate** of adequate size with map scale information and a small magnifier.

Check out the compass before taking it out in the field. Make sure the red needle points north. That sounds really elementary, but I have found two quality compasses where the needle was painted wrong, and the red needle pointed *south!*

Basic Land Navigation: How to Set a Compass Bearing

You need to know this basic land navigation technique, whether you are in the wilderness or in a city.

One of the simplest methods to keep going in a straight line. To keep from traveling in circles is to learn how to take a bearing.

To sight or take a bearing do the following:

1. Using the owner's manual, adjust the compass for declination.
2. While holding the compass at waist level, turn squarely toward a distant object. Hold the compass so that the direction of travel arrow points directly at the object. (Point the direction of travel arrow away from you; perpendicular to your body.)
3. While holding the compass, turn the compass housing (the dial) and align the orienting arrow (engraved in the rotating housing) underneath the red magnetic needle.

The bearing data is found where the direction of travel arrow intersects the compass housing. At this point the hiker can walk towards the object (e.g., a mountain peak, a building, etc.) on a bearing. While heading out on the new bearing, consider walking to an object that is in-line with the destination. For example, perhaps there is a distinctive tree or rock outcropping halfway between the hiker and the destination. Simply verify the bearing to the object and walk directly towards it and place the compass in a pocket. Homing in on an intermediate object prevents fixation on the compass and keeps the navigation simple.

Consider using multiple intermediate bearings in route. Remember, a quality topographic map should always be taken into the field with the compass.

An excellent reference book is *Staying Found: The Complete Map and Compass Handbook* by June Fleming. This is my go-to land navigation reference book.

Do You Need a Gun?

Few actions require more forethought than purchasing a firearm. But more important than the style, caliber, action, and size of the gun is the reason for buying one in the first place.

Why do you want a firearm? Do you really need it? Would you be better off without a gun? You might be surprised.

Suppose you have no firearms background whatsoever, but you want to be prepared for emergencies, and are considering buying one. Maybe you've seen some of the TV shows where preppers are armed and their primary focus seems to be the inevitable gunfight that will happen when the Stuff Hits the Fan. Or, let's say you are concerned about self-defense, and want to be able to protect yourself and your family. As a side benefit, you may want to eventually get into hunting, or think it might be a good idea to learn how to shoot accurately.

Well, don't just go buy something that goes "bang" before giving it some thought. And you may decide you are better off without a gun.

For me, not owning firearms was never even a consideration. I come from a long line of hunters and shooters, and some of our firearms have been passed down for generations. I grew up on an Iowa farm, and all my peers hunted. Some of my first memories include my dad teaching me gun safety and how to shoot. The first item I ever saved up to buy was a Ruger 10/22 rifle.

In my Dad's locked gun cabinet were firearms of many configurations, ranging from pistols to shotguns. Dad, a World War II infantryman, had an M1 Carbine, and a couple loaded magazines. That was the weapon he reached for when things went bump in the night on the farm. It never occurred to me to use that M1 "assault rifle" with the extended magazines to do harm to anyone.

Here are some of my opinions, based on experience, which will hopefully impact your decision process:

- I believe in the Second Amendment right to bear arms. But I don't think everyone should own a firearm. Anyone unwilling

You shouldn't just go out and buy a gun. This rifle (top) and handgun have very different applications and uses.

to invest the necessary time to become proficient with a firearm, could become a danger to himself or others. A person who is mentally unstable, a convicted felon, or otherwise legally not eligible should not own a firearm.

- Before you buy any firearm, take a gun and/or hunter safety course or a concealed weapons class, even if you don't intend to carry a concealed firearm. There are many educational opportunities available and contacting the sheriff or your local Fish and Game Department is a good way to locate a class. Have a safe, secure place to store the firearm and ammunition before you go shopping.
- Why are you buying a gun? Self-defense? Hunting? Recreation? Target shooting? Learn the differences between firearms—a .38 caliber snubbie revolver for self-defense will not work very well for deer hunting. And that scoped, bolt action hunting rifle might not be the best choice to repel intruders inside your apartment.

Here are some things to think about as part of the firearms-buying decision process:

Where will you secure the gun? Owning a gun that can't be stored safely is irresponsible. In my view, that is a good reason *not* to have one.

A firearm is neither good nor evil. It is an unthinking machine until someone picks it up and decides how it will be used. This can be for evil or for good, depending on the user. Possessing a gun won't keep you safe. Like anything, you must develop the skills to use the weapon.

A semi-automatic weapon with high capacity magazine does not make the best self-defense weapon. Large capacity magazines encourage a lot of "spray-and-pray" in my honest opinion, and the only shots that count are the ones that hit the intended target.

Flashback: A few years ago as a reporter for a newspaper in Oregon, I interviewed US Marine Kyle Thompson of La Pine, Oregon. Thompson had just come back from deployments in Iraq and Afghanistan, where he had served on Recon teams. The Marines, all of whom were sniper school graduates, were frequently dropped in Taliban territory to track down terrorist bands and help defend isolated villages.

With any weapon at their disposal, Thompson said some of the Marines frequently relied on the bolt action, .308-caliber M-24 scoped sniper rifle. The Taliban were armed with fully-automatic AK-47s. A common ambush situation, Thompson said, was that a Taliban terrorist would open up on a patrol and empty a thirty-round magazine in a continuous burst. The Marines could stay out of AK range and respond with an M-24.

Probably the most important self-defense question is this: Are you willing to kill someone to keep yourself or loved ones safe? This question needs to be answered honestly before you go any further on the self-defense firearms purchasing path.

In his book *On Killing*, Lieutenant Colonel Dave Grossman argues that many people could not kill someone, even when threatened with lethal force. Killing from a distance, Grossman writes, such as artillery or bombing, can be relatively easy. But a close encounter, where you can see the other person and witness the impact of pulling the trigger, he comments, can be extremely difficult for most people.

Your unwillingness or inability to use your gun under dire circumstances could cause you to be disarmed. Then you have armed a perpetrator.

If your mind is not made up on any of these points, don't buy a gun. It will do you no good and may cause harm.

Top Three Firearms for Beginners

I like and enjoy shooting anything that goes "boom," with a special affinity for traditional black powder long rifles. Every year, time permitting, I hunt elk, deer, upland game, waterfowl, and whatever else I can legally pursue. But I try to stay away from writing about firearms. There is so much of it on the Internet, both good and B.S., that anything I contribute will be adding another drop to an already overflowing bucket.

But the question remains. So, here are my top three long gun choices for people starting out. You need:

1. **A .22 caliber rifle**
2. **A shotgun**
3. **A centerfire hunting rifle**

You can worry about handguns, black rifles, and tactical guns later, once you get the basics.

Also, variations of these three basic firearms are easy to find. If you shop around and watch for sales, you may be able to acquire all three of the suggested firearms for under $1000.

The top three cartridge and caliber choices for newcomers are the .22 caliber Long Rifle, a twenty or twelve-gauge shotgun and a centerfire rifle.

If you don't have any firearms, what should you buy and what do you need? Here's where to start building your bushcraft battery:

1. **.22 caliber rifle:** Everybody needs a .22. A beginner needs a manageable rifle to start out with, one that doesn't belt them in the chops every time they pull the trigger. A .22 allows a person to learn the basics of marksmanship, which will transfer over to centerfire rifles and other firearms. For the beginner, a .22 is perfect. It has no kick, is low noise, and ammunition is frequently on sale.

   In addition to target practice, a .22 could be used for self-defense. In the hands of a cool marksman who places his shot correctly, a .22 rifle can take down deer or larger game. Pick the action you like best, but some experienced shooters recommend getting the same action in your .22 as with your centerfire hunting rifle, so the muscle memory and training carries over.

   Get your young folks, girls and boys, wives and sisters, brother-in-laws and uncles out in the fields and teach them safety and respect for this dangerous piece of survival equipment. Enroll them in NRA safety classes and help them build confidence to last a lifetime.

2. **Shotgun:** A shotgun can be a close-range weapon and a tool for harvesting small game. But properly loaded with buckshot or a slug, a well-aimed shotgun can put down any big game animal in the western hemisphere. For the newcomer, the choice of gauge narrows down to twelve-gauge or the smaller twenty gauge. Any of the less common gauges might make it harder to find cheap ammunition.

3. **Bolt action centerfire rifle:** I like bolt action rifles and have hunted with them all my life. Even in the thickets of Mississippi while hunting deer, I never felt handicapped with the slower operating bolt action, as opposed to a pump or semi-automatic.

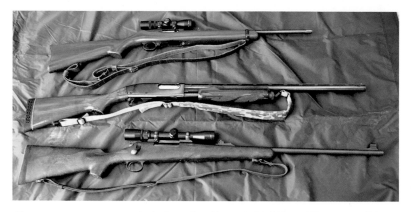

These are my personal choices for those initial three firearms. (From top) Ruger 10/22, Remington 870 Pump shotgun in twelve-gauge, and Remington 700 in seven-millimeter Remington Magnum.

The bolt action is the choice of many top snipers and marksmen, and in addition to being a fantastic hunting rifle, the bolt action also tends to be very accurate. My personal choices for the beginner battery are the Ruger 10/22 .22 caliber semi-automatic; a 20 or 12 gauge Remington 870 pump shotgun; and a scoped, bolt-action Remington 700. Here's why:

1. **Ruger 10/22:** I bought my Ruger in 1966, when I was fourteen, at Red Fox Sporting Goods, in Boone, Iowa. The Ruger cost fifty-four dollars, and I worked fifty-four hours, chopping corn and weeds out of bean fields to buy it.

   Since then, I have shot tens of thousands of rounds through that little carbine. Plinking at targets was one of my favorite pastimes when I was a kid. I also shot rats at the dump and hunted small game extensively. While I frequently rely on iron sights on other traditional-styled rifles, I like a four-power telescopic sight on my .22. In brush, the magnification allows you to see holes in the foliage to shoot through. The scope helps the shooter place his shots more accurately and efficiently.

2. **Remington 870:** If I could only have one gun (perish the thought!) it would be a twelve-gauge Remington 870 pump shotgun. Properly loaded, this gun can put down anything from flying doves to big bears.

It would be my weapon of choice in virtually any close range gunfight, and it is the weapon I reach for when things go bump in the night. This classic American-made pump shotgun has sold over four million copies, and is the issue shotgun for many law enforcement and military agencies. A twelve-gauge is the standard gauge, but for small-framed people a twenty-gauge might be a better choice.

In 1982, I bought my first 870, a twelve-gauge, for hunting deer with buckshot or slugs in the thick brush of Mississippi. That gun got used hard during all hunting seasons. It was also my waterfowl gun, and never failed in the mud, water, cattails, and swamps. I liked it so much, I later bought a twenty gauge 870 Wingmaster for hunting upland game. Then I bought a synthetic-stocked 870 twelve-gauge for my son. He can use any of my guns for hunting, but prefers the black one because of its appearance.

There are any number of aftermarket upgrades that can make the 870 look badder and more tactical. But as a perpetrator deterrent, nothing quite matches the 870's signature "slicky-slick" of a round being chambered.

3. **Remington 700:** This bolt action rifle uses the same basic action as the US military's M-24 sniper rifle. I own a model BDL in 7mm-08 for deer, and a synthetic Remington 700 in 7 mm Remington Magnum for elk and everything else.

I also own other bolt actions, including a Ruger Mark V in .223. A Winchester 670 went through my hands a few years back. My brother Mike's Winchester pre-64 Model 70 remains one of the most accurate 30.06s I've ever fired.

No American manufacturer can afford to make a shoddy, junky

bolt action centerfire rifle. If you have a favorite major manufacturer, stick with them and you won't go wrong.

As far as a caliber goes, find one you can shoot, and that the ammunition will be easy to find. The .308 and .223 are military rounds and the ammunition is common and cheap. A 30.06 is never a mistake.

For a slight framed person, the light kicking .223 or .243 will be good calibers to start with.

I'm sure my personal list will cause debate. (And isn't that half the fun?) But I believe we can all agree on this: Before you buy any firearm, get some training so you are able to handle it safely. Have the means to secure the firearm in your home and always treat every gun as if it was loaded!

Remember This:

Survival gear and tools run the gamut from water bottles to firearms. Each has a specific task or job to perform, and you want to have everything covered. Think about what items are easiest to acquire, which ones might be the most challenging, and plan accordingly. Your tools need to be individualized, and you should practice using them before they are needed.

CHAPTER 7
MAKING A FIRE

The ability to start a fire can save your life. The inability to start a fire can cost it.

Some unknown individual, eons ago, figured out that fire was a good thing. It could keep them warm, cook food, provide light, scare off predators, and serve as a social center.

Today, a campfire can still create a community. People want to sit around it. Conversation naturally follows. Fire-making may be one of the most important bushcraft skills you learn.

Choose the Best Ignition System

In elk hunting, it's always the hope of bagging one that sucks us hunters out in crappy weather into remote mountainous areas.

Flashback: The day was bitterly cold in Idaho's Selway wilderness, the snow was knee deep, and there were miles between us and the nearest road. If there was an emergency, we would have to make a fire, then one of us would go for help. I always carried survival gear, and was confident of my ability to use it effectively.

The temperatures were frigid all day, and they continued dropping as dusk came. A canteen on the outside of a daypack froze solid. The only way to stay warm was to keep moving. We got back to camp after dark. The first order of business was to start the fire. I took out my waterproof match container and tried to light a strike-anywhere match on the side. All the matches had been replaced a couple months ago at the start of hunting season, but not one of the twenty in the container would light. Then I tried the backup butane lighter in my pack. Because of the cold, it didn't work either. Luckily, we had fire starter and backup matches at camp that did work, and the fire was soon thawing us out.

"So suppose one of us had gotten hurt and couldn't move—what would we have done to start a fire?" I asked my hunting partner. We agreed it could have been fatal.

That frigid hunt was in 1993, and for years afterward, I experimented to find a reliable firemaking method.

In 2002, as part of a research project for Boy Scout Troop 18 in Bend, Oregon, Dr. Jim Grenfell and I set out to find the ultimate, practical fire ignition method that would work for the average person. Jim was a retired college instructor, but had been a fighter pilot during the Korean War. He had graduated from three of the Air Force's survival schools, and like me, had this compulsion to find the most effective survival fire starting method.

Criteria to be tested were: ease of operation, ability to use one-handed (in the event of an injury), reliability, widespread availability, durability, practicality, and ease of carry. We ruled out any items that seemed to rely on expensive, gee-whiz technology.

Over the course of the next several months, we laboriously tested and re-tested conventional fire making methods. When something showed promise after initial experiments, we turned the scouts loose on it. If the method survived that torture test, we'd ask average outdoors people to try and then comment on the materials.

Here's what we found:

Bow drill, hand drill, or other primitive wood friction methods: These were not even in the running. In a survival situation, you need to make a fire quickly. With the primitive friction methods, you must have the time to make a system and the skills to use it. You'd also have to find the correct dry materials to build the setup.

The people who depended on the friction method for twirling up a fire probably carried their own specialized sticks with them. Even in a forest, there might not be dry, suitable materials to build a setup. If rubbing two sticks together to create fire was easy, or even just moderately difficult, people would never have developed ways to carry a live coal between camps! We decided the best place to use the primitive methods was in front of the blazing campfire, for demonstration purposes.

Matches: In the best case scenario you should be able to make one fire with every match, right?

That points out a real problem with matches: there is a finite number of them, and when they're gone, you're out of luck. And what if all the matches are used up to make one fire because of a low skill level?

Every brand and type of match we tried was unreliable as a survival tool. But if forced to make a recommendation, I'd say the best choice is REI Stormproof Matches. They work well under many adverse circumstances, but you can only carry a few (ten, with striker strip) in a standard match case.

The advantage is that most people can strike a match, and have a general idea of how to use them.

The disadvantage is that matches deteriorate over time and fail, even if they're waterproof. While coating the heads with paraffin or other sealants will work for a while, that doesn't make the matches dependable. Most regular book matches are useless if damp, or if they're even exposed to moisture.

Another critical aspect is the abrasive strip on the match box or book. If it gets damp, wet or worn out, the matches won't work. And one brand of match may not ignite on another's abrasive strip! Even strike-anywhere matches don't necessarily light when struck on an abrasive surface. Try standing in knee-deep snow during a snow and sleet storm and finding a dry, abrasive surface to strike a match on!

Butane lighter: I carry a butane lighter in my pants pocket, another in my jacket pocket, and a third in my pack. If a quick fire is needed, the idea is to flick a BIC and get the job done. A standard BIC lighter, according to my tests, will have about an hour's worth of flame in it. But I don't trust *any* butane lighter, and you shouldn't either.

The Achilles heel of the butane lighter is temperature. The boiling point of Butane is approximately -0.5 C at sea level. (This boiling point will drop with an increase in altitude given the reduced pressure.) This means that as the lighter nears freezing, less gas will be vaporized inside of the lighter and will make it hard to light. And the higher in elevation you are, the less chance you have for ignition!

My experiments show that placing a butane lighter in ice water (thirty-three degrees Fahrenheit) disables it almost instantaneously. If the lighter is removed from a one-minute ice water bath, and placed in a seventy degree area, several minutes will pass before it is warm enough to function.

This time varies on the size, brand, and make of the lighter. If you warm the lighter in your already warm hand, it can take at least ninety seconds under ideal conditions, and probably closer to four minutes, to make it functional.

So, if you fall into an icy river, wade to shore, and desperately need to make a warm-up fire, your butane lighter won't work for what seems like an eternity. In a situation where your hands are freezing, you may not be able to warm the lighter quickly. Your cold, numb fingers may not be able to work the wheel, either. By the time the lighter is warm enough to ignite, you may not be able to use it.

Any lighter's durability is suspect. All it takes is one grain of sand in the wrong place and the machinery is disabled. And don't forget that if you inadvertently drop your butane lighter into a campfire, an explosion will probably follow!

Zippo-style lighters: For a while, this appeared to be the winner. I filled my Zippo with lighter fluid to the saturation point, then sat down to see how many fires it would make before it failed. Over the next two days, (this is probably a comment on my social life), the total number of lights was 974!

When full of fluid, the Zippo worked immediately after a one-minute ice water bath. It came out the freezer overnight and fired on the second try. I sealed the hinge and opening with a piece of duct tape, left it alone for a month, and it still fired.

But the Zippo-style lighter was wildly inconsistent in other areas. A fully saturated lighter dried out completely in my pocket in three days in the desert. Having it sealed didn't matter. And sometimes, for reasons I couldn't figure out, the Zippo just wouldn't light.

While you can fuel a Zippo with gasoline if need be, don't rely on one as your only ignition source.

Magnesium block: A favorite of the survival shows, the magnesium block with a ferrocerium rod on top has some merit. The idea is to shave off pieces of magnesium into a small pile, then ignite it with a spark from the flint stick. The magnesium block is waterproof.

The problem with the system is that it takes a long time to scrape enough shavings off the block to ignite, and it's really easy to scatter the pile if you bump it or the wind comes up. A magnesium block is okay, but not your best choice.

Ferro rods or sticks: I carry a ferrocerium stick on my keyring and have several in different parts of my gear. When used in combination with cotton balls saturated with petroleum jelly, the system is nearly foolproof. Put the cotton balls in a plastic case or Ziploc bag.

But it takes some effort to learn how to use ferro rods or sticks and like anything, there is no substitute for practice. Using a flint stick with only one hand can be done, but not as easily as using a butane lighter.

At the end of all this research, Grenfell and I concluded that there is no ultimate firemaking tool, and you should never rely on just one type.

My Recommendation for Starting a Fire

Take at least three different methods because environmental factors might disable one ignition solution and then you'll have two back-ups. Include a fire starting tool out of each of the following categories:

I'd stake my life on this collection of fire starters. (From bottom, going clockwise) Stormproof matches (stored in a waterproof container, with the abrasive strip that comes with them), BIC mini butane lighter, ferrocerium rod with cotton balls and petroleum jelly, charcloth, waxed firestarter, and Zippo lighter.

- **Ferro stick, cotton balls, and petroleum jelly:** If forced to pick just one method of firemaking, this would be it. With practice, the combination is quick and reliable. But without a lot of practice and experimenting, you probably won't be able to use it with one hand. If you're disabled, nearly unconscious, or untrained, you might not be able to figure out how it works.
- **Butane lighter:** If you're lucky and can keep your lighter warm and dry, a butane lighter may take care of all your firemaking needs. Many kids can't operate a butane lighter without practice, though, so some training may be needed with your juvenile outdoor partners.
- **Stormproof matches:** Most folks don't need instruction on how to light a match, so it's a good idea to include matches with your gear. Invest in premium matches that have the best chance of working when you need them and rotate your stock regularly. Be sure to take along the abrasive strip from the match box and store all matches in a waterproof container!

No matter which firemaking methods you use, take along charcloth (see text below for instruction on how to create charcloth) and firestarter in a waterproof plastic bag. If your Zippo or butane lighter leaks or runs out of fuel, you can use the wheel and flint to make a spark that can be caught on a piece of charcloth. Also, any other ignition methods that involve sparks can be used with charcloth. Firestarter should be compact, durable, and easy to carry. It can make the difference between dying of hypothermia or getting a fire going with damp tinder and kindling!

One last suggestion: *Include a road flare in your survival gear.* It is a fantastic signaling tool, burns for at least fifteen minutes and will ignite virtually anything!

Make Simple, Effective Fire Starters

You must have an effective ignition system to turn a tiny spark into a sustainable fire for warmth. However, while most people can start a small flame, they don't have the skills or supplies to sustain it. Firestarters are materials that will sustain a flame for several minutes, allowing you to add fuels that will build the fire. Those materials must be included in your firemaking kits.

I learned this while covering Search and Rescue missions as a newspaper reporter for the Bend, Oregon *Bulletin.* The Deschutes County SAR team is one of the busiest in the nation because of the influx of tourists every year who underestimate the wilderness and the potential danger.

One particular incident stuck in my mind.

Flashback: Several visitors rented snowmobiles and took off for a quick ride. A storm came up, they became lost, and their machines got bogged down in the waist-deep snow. They tried to start a fire to stay warm, but couldn't get one going. In desperation, they tried to light the nylon tow rope, the titles to the snowmobiles, credit cards, and finally paper money. They completely ignored the gasoline in the tank, and didn't know how to find the dry wood or other natural firestarter that was all around them in the pine forest.

They never did get any fire going and they might have died if the temperatures had dropped much lower. I wondered—how expensive was that bushcraft lesson compared to the cash they tried to burn?

Some of the most effective firestarters can be made at home. Here are some that can be made with items you probably already have.

Foil: I always carry foil in my mini survival kit, and it is very useful for starting fires in snow or on wet ground. The foil tops of yogurt containers are perfect. The foil will help keep that initial flame off the snow or wet ground.

Gasoline and matches are one of the deadliest combinations in bushcrafting firestarting.

Never, never, never pour gasoline on a smoldering campfire. The gas will ignite instantly, and the flame may follow the stream up to the gas and cause it to explode. Besides, pouring gas on a pile of wood and tossing a match on top is no guarantee that the wood will ignite. If the wood is green or wet, or the firewood has not been arranged correctly, the flames may burn until the gas evaporates and then go out.

However, if you must use the gas-match combination, here the safest, most effective way to make that work:

1. Take a piece of aluminum foil and make it into a small cup. Pour a teaspoon of gas into the depression.
2. *Put the gas can a long way from the ignition source.*
3. Light the gas with a ferro rod, and place kindling on top of the flame. The gas will burn for several minutes and if you have your kindling and firewood squared away, you should have no problem lighting the fire.
4. You will use a fraction of the gas, there shouldn't be an explosion, and the gas will burn for several minutes.

Waxed cotton cloth: That snowmobile incident started me thinking about finding a lightweight, compact firestarter that could be carried

The charcloth (top) and waxed fire starter should be enough to start a fire.

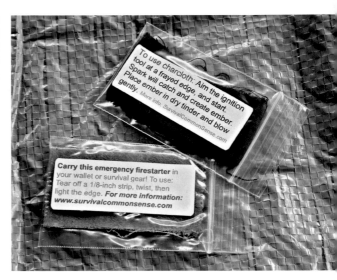

To use charcloth: Aim the ignition tool at a frayed edge, and start. Spark will catch and create ember. Place ember in dry tinder and blow gently. More info: SurvivalCommonSense.com

Carry this emergency firestarter in your wallet or survival gear! To use: Tear off a 1/8-inch strip, twist, then light the edge. **For more information:** www.survivalcommonsense.com

easily. It had to be reliable, and most importantly, fit in a wallet credit card slot.

So, I experimented with one hundred percent cotton cloth and candle wax combinations and came up with a firestarter that is about the size of a credit card. I carry a piece in my wallet, and every bushcraft kit I have. The cloth is dipped in melted wax and then dried. The finished firestarter is put in a plastic bag. This stuff, like any wax candle, will melt in hot weather. Don't leave it on a car dashboard or with your gear where it might be exposed to high temperatures. The wallet firestarter is completely waterproof, and won't absorb moisture.

Another effective fire starter is to partially dip a one hundred percent cotton makeup removal pad in paraffin. When you need to light it, fluff up the non-coated part of the pad and light it with a ferrocerium rod. Carry this in a plastic bag to keep the wax from melting and the non-treated cotton dry.

Cotton balls and petroleum jelly: This is my go-to firestarter that goes in every kit. The cotton balls are infused with the jelly. The easiest way to make these is to put a big gob of the jelly in a plastic bag, along with several cotton balls, and massage the jelly into the cotton.

A good container for the infused cotton balls are prescription drug bottles. Everybody has a prescription for something, and the bottles can be recycled into fire starter containers. The bottles will also hold matches and a variety of other small useful items.

Cotton balls cost less than a penny each, and five will fill a standard prescription bottle. An added benefit is that cotton balls are sterile and could be used as part of a first aid kit. This incredibly effective firestarter costs pennies to make, lasts forever, and is so handy that it can be carried everywhere easily. Chapstick, and other such products with beeswax in them, also may ignite when rubbed on cotton balls.

Pitchwood: Also commonly known as "fatwood," "fat lighter," "lighter wood," "rich lighter," "pine knot," "lighter knot," or "heart pine." Pitchwood can be found in virtually every pine forest.

Pine trees produce resin, or pitch, to defend against wounds or insect attack. When the bark is wounded, the tree pumps out resin to protect the wound from fungal attack or to expel an offending insect. The pine resin is also highly flammable.

Over time, as the heartwood forms with age, excess resin is pushed into the wood in the center of the tree. Eventually, this resin can totally permeate the heartwood and create a "pitch soaked" condition. This resin concentration creates a very decay-resistant heartwood. If the tree dies and falls over, the sapwood (the living, functioning part of the wood), rots fairly rapidly. However, the pitch-soaked heart can last for decades.

This resin-impregnated heartwood becomes hard and rot-resistant. It may be found on the forest floor, and it will easily light. I frequently scrape the pitchwood with a knife and then ignite the scrapings with a ferro rod.

One of the easiest places to find pitchwood is in a dead branch on a live tree, next to the trunk.

The sap is highly flammable and can easily be found near a wound on a pine tree.

Don't use dryer lint: This material comes from the lint filter of a dryer and some folks think it is an effective firestarter. I don't. I won't carry it and I recommend you don't either.

If the lint comes from a load of one hundred percent cotton items, the lint may ignite readily. But if the dryer load is of mixed fabrics, such as wool, rayon, or polyester, the lint *may* not light at all. Besides, dryer lint may also have dog hair, dirt, pollen, and other substances in it. Proponents claim dryer lint is free and effective. But this is false economy. If saving money is your concern, shouldn't you be drying your clothes on a line outside?

If you must carry dryer lint, test every batch before including it with your gear.

Regardless of what fire starter you decide to take with you, take something. And practice using it beforehand to be prepared for when you need an emergency fire.

How to Make Charcloth

Every emergency kit should include charcloth. It is a necessity, in my opinion, for any survival fire making system. Charcloth is easy to make, and is a good project to do while sitting around the campfire at night. Here is why you need some.

Charcloth is a material that catches sparks. The organic material is "cooked" at a high temperature in an airless container with an exhaust hole, whereby the cloth is changed through a process called pyrolysis. The charred cloth becomes a source of fuel with a very low ignition temperature.

Properly made charcloth will easily catch a spark that will then grow into an ember. This ember can be transferred to a tinder bundle and blown into a flame.

The concept is nothing new. Flint and steel fire making is one of the oldest and most efficient methods of starting a fire known to man. I imagine some ancient ancestors figured out that smacking iron pyrite rocks together made sparks. The logical progression would be to figure out some way to catch those sparks. As soon as someone found a way to grow those sparks into embers, a whole new world opened up.

Since the only source of light and heat at night was a campfire, and the only way to cook was over embers, making a fire was paramount to survival in colder climates. Being able to reliably make fire every night meant the tribes could venture further north into colder climates to follow game herds.

I think those ancient charred materials evolved into today's charcloth. It is every bit as valuable to the modern bushcrafter as it used to be way back when.

Charcloth can be used to catch a spark off a disabled but sparking lighter. Matches are always suspect, and a match might become damp and spark without lighting. In those cases, charcloth can catch the spark from the struck match.

Probably the most important attribute of charcloth is that it is windproof. A match or lighter may be blown out. But once a spark lands on charcloth, blowing on it makes the ember grow faster.

Once you discover how easy it is to make charcloth, there will never be an excuse for running out, or not having some in your survival kit.

Here are the items needed to make charcloth, and what you need to do:

Container: A regular-sized Altoids or other brand of mint tin can, with a small hole punched in the top. A small nail works well to make the hole in the lid. Ideally, the tin would be airtight except for the small hole, but that is not a deal breaker.

Charcloth can be made using aluminum foil. Wrap the cloth or organic material tightly in the foil and poke a hole in it for ventilation.

What if you have a tin or container, but no lid? Can you still make charcloth?

Sure. Put the material to be charred in the bottom of the can, and cover it up with an inch or so of ash or dirt. All you need to do is assure the material cooks without igniting.

Charring material: There are many natural, organic materials that can be charred. These include some tree barks, grasses, fungi, or rotted wood. Depending on where you live, there will probably be some natural material that will work well.

Charcloth is easy to make. All you need is a tin with a lid with a hole punched in the top. Fill the container with the material to be charred, and place on a heat source. The material will heat up, and the smoke coming out of the hole will ignite. When the flame dies down, remove and let cool completely.

Experimenting with charring different natural materials is fun, and finding these is a great outdoor activity for kids.

Cloth: I like making charcloth, since it is a good way to use up or recycle scrap material. Stay away from any cloth blend that has synthetics in it; the plastic may melt without catching the spark. Wool is naturally fire resistant, so don't use that either.

Cotton denim from old Wranglers or Levi 501s or work jeans works very well, and that cloth is my go-to favorite. An old pair of worn-out jeans can provide enough charring material to last for a long time. Denim is always a good choice because there is never a shortage of old jeans! Other one hundred percent cotton items can also be used. One hundred percent cotton insulated underwear is excellent for this project. If you have to buy material to char, get Monk's Cloth. The loosely-woven, one hundred percent cotton makes great charcloth. I don't wear cotton clothing on hikes or canoe trips, but I always carry several cotton bandanas. Strips off these make excellent charring materials as well.

Heat source: Don't make charcloth inside. The process is really smoky, and you'll set off any smoke alarm in the house. The smoke doesn't smell good, and the stench will permeate the interior of your home.

A campfire or outdoor grill works fine. I use my double burner propane stove outside.

What to do:

1. Tear the cloth into strips that will fit into the charring tin and place it on the heat source. In about five to ten minutes the tin will start to smoke. In a few more minutes, the smoke plume will ignite. Let the flame burn. Then adjust the heat, if possible, so the flame stays about two-to-four inches high.

2. When the flame dies down, and the smoke lessens, take the can from the fire and *let it cool completely*. When you open the can, check the charcloth to make sure it is completely black and somewhat flexible.

3. If you've used the can without a lid, and topped it with dirt or ash, wait until the smoke stops and the can cools, checking the charcloth.

4. Let the charcloth cool completely, then store it in a plastic bag or some sort of container. As long as it is not flexed or moved a great deal, the material will last for years.

A char tin should be metal with a top. A hole will be punched in the top to let out smoke.

Fill the tin with strips of one hundred percent cotton cloth. Loosely pack the material.

Cook the filled tin outside. The smoke will ignite. When the flame dies down, take the tin off the heat source and let it cool completely.

The finished charcloth should be completely black and slightly flexible. When done correctly, the finished charcloth should easily catch a spark and grow into an ember.

I carry a small piece of charcloth in my wallet, and in the zippered compartment of my survival belt. Once you learn how to make charcloth, you won't want to be without it!

Find Dry Tinder Anywhere

Flashback: The rain dripped off the brim of my hat, and wind gusts threatened to blow out any ignition attempts. I was in the Oregon high desert, and attempting to demonstrate starting a one-match fire in the rain to a group of Boy Scouts.

The circumstances were challenging. It had rained on and off for a couple of days and everything was soaked. But a juniper tree was handy, and you couldn't ask for a better source of fire starting materials if you knew where to look. (According to *Merriam-Webster's Collegiate Dictionary*, tinder is, "a very flammable substance adaptable for use as kindling." The dictionary says kindling is, "easily combustible material for starting a fire.")

I looked for the dry side of the tree, stripped off the outer bark, and quickly gathered the fine, dry, inner bark. It went in my pocket to keep it dry. Then my son Dan, about twelve at the time, piped up.

"A match? Seriously, Dad?" he commented. "Aren't you going to use flint and steel?"

Actually, in those windy conditions, the old-time firemaking method is more efficient than a match. Although a match might blow out in the wind, once a spark from the flint and steel is caught in the charcloth, the wind only increases the ember's growth.

The dry tinder was formed into a ball about the size of my fist. I caught the spark on the charcloth, placed it in the middle of the bundle which then quickly ignited. Secretly, I was kind of impressed, too!

A very important bushcraft skill is knowing how and where to find dry materials to start a fire. This can be a seasonal thing. In the Oregon high desert during the winter months, starting a campfire can be a real challenge. During the summer fire season, the challenge is to keep a fire from starting and spreading out of control.

Tinder can be virtually anything—pine needles, leaves, bark, dead weeds and vines, etc. The most important aspect is that the tinder is dry and very finely textured, to more easily catch fire.

In an urban setting, a warming fire might be needed if a disaster happens that damages the road infrastructure, the power goes out, and people are stranded in a parking lot. In that situation, a fire might be every bit as important as it usually is in the wilderness.

In reality, dry tinder can be found in virtually every area, if you know the general areas to search. Here are some things to look for.

Dry is the most important part of the equation. Obviously, damp, green, or wet materials won't ignite easily, if at all.

Out of the wind is the first area to look for. This is easy to see—look at which way the wind blows, then see where you'd have to go to get out of it. On a tree trunk, the area that is out of the wind is also going to be the dry side. Start your search there.

Off the ground is also an important factor. Most of the wood found on the ground will be damp or rotten. Neither will start very well. While you might find several inches of leaves or pine needles on the forest floor, they might be too damp to light. Dead pine needles still on the tree might be an excellent choice.

The dry side of this tree is easy to find. Look for the area of the tree that is out of the wind.

That goes for some grasses or reeds, too. Standing, dead stalks may be dry enough to ignite.

Find pitchwood in most pine forests. Pitchwood, the resinous wood of coniferous trees, is highly flammable and easily found.

Find a dead limb on a live conifer, and there might be pitchwood in the branch, next to the trunk.

Cattails, milkweed, and thistle down can be found in season. They are usually located on a stalk and can easily be harvested. The seeds are attached to downy parachutes and are dispersed by the wind. They won't last long once they get fluffy, so gather all you can when you find them.

A piece of firewood might be all you have to work with. In that case, the piece might need to be split, or batoned, with a knife into smaller pieces. Done correctly, batoning is not going to hurt a knife.

Basically, batoning is splitting wood with a knife. Start with a straight-grained piece of firewood, about twelve to eighteen inches long. Place the knife edge with the grain, and hammer it with another piece of wood. Split the pieces further into smaller chunks until there are fine splinters that will catch fire readily.

Batoning should be viewed as a last resort, and it isn't a good idea to use a folder knife for this. Rather than risk breaking your best survival tool, carry an ax or hatchet if you anticipate having difficulties finding dry wood.

Make a feather stick out of one of these batoned pieces or a dry limb. This is a great activity for newcomers just learning safe knife handling. Whittle long, fine shavings on the stick, but don't detach them. After a few accumulate, the wood starts to resemble a feather. Several of these will make a good starter for the campfire.

If you are in an urban emergency situation, start your search for tinder and flammable materials in the nearest dumpster or trash can.

Just because the woods or parking lot are wet, that doesn't mean you can't get a warming fire started. Look around, and think, "Dry, out of the wind, and off the ground." You should find something that can start a campfire.

Ten Steps to Build a Campfire

When it comes to bushcraft fire building, the initial ignition seems to get the limelight, while building the actual campfire tends to be glossed over. The truth is that ignition is incredibly important, but creating the campfire requires skill, too.

Every fire has three main components: oxygen, fuel, and ignition. If one of these is missing the fire won't catch. Make sure all these items are present before attempting to start a campfire.

A campfire can provide heat, light, and a way to cook food. Knowing how to build one under extreme conditions is an incredibly valuable survival skill.

Here are ten steps to build a campfire:

1. **Location, location, location:** Look for the spot that will be the safest and that will allow the fire to work most effectively. A reflector, such as a rock or stack of logs, can greatly increase the heat value.

   A really effective way to reflect heat is to build the fire between a large rock and the sitting area. A tarp, placed at a forty-five-degree angle to the fire, behind your seat, can reflect a lot of heat. Get out of the wind if possible.

   Take a good look around, and don't forget to look up. Make sure there are no widow makers, snags, or loose rocks that might fall on the fire or you. Snow on an overhead branch, for example, might melt from the fire's heat and put out the flames. (Read Jack London's *To Build a Fire* for a really good example of what not to do.)

2. **Clear an area around where the fire will be:** A good rule of thumb is to clear an area at least ten feet in diameter around the actual fire. Fire rings made of stones can help contain the fire. Don't use rocks from a stream bed—they may have moisture in them, and the heat may create steam that will cause the rocks to explode.

3. **Check the wind:** The wind should blow the initial flame into the tinder bundle and the rest of the wood. The wind can also carry the smoke in a certain area, and sparks from the campfire might ignite flammable materials downwind. Make sure the wind is blowing in a safe direction.

4. **Know where to look for dry, dead wood:** Basically, look off the ground and find dry sticks on trees and bushes. You may need to whittle off the wet outer layer.

5. **Practice with your ignition method:** Make sure they will work. An emergency situation is not the time for on-the-job training. Be familiar with your favorite method of starting a flame.

   For example, just because you have matches, doesn't mean you will be able to start a fire with them. The wind might blow them out, or your skill level might not be good enough to light a fire with one match.

6. **Carry fire starter and different methods of starting a flame:** I always carry matches, a BIC Mini butane lighter, a ferrocerium rod, and traditional flint and steel. One of these methods should work, regardless of the situation.

But ninety-nine percent of the time, I make a campfire using primitive methods. This saves the emergency tools for emergencies. Besides, the primitive methods allow me to practice my skills, are a lot of fun, and I enjoy teaching beginners the techniques.

7. **Make a tinder bundle:** The tinder bundle is essentially a nest of very flammable materials that will ignite easily. It is where the initial match, glowing charcloth, or spark from a ferrocerium rod would go. This bundle will light easily and flare up quickly.

8. **Gather wood and stage it:** The wood should be piled according to size, and placed in piles, ready to add to the flame:

- **Tinder bundle and fire starter:** This is the fuel that is fine-textured and easily lighted from a single match or flame from a lighter. As a minimum, get enough tinder to fill your hat. (People always ask how much is enough. A hat-full is enough.)
- **Intermediate:** This wood is pencil-sized and larger, up to about an inch in diameter. When the tinder is going well, this wood is added.
- **Firewood:** This goes from wrist-sized on up. This is the wood that will produce the heat and coals for cooking, heating, and light.

9. **Stack the wood correctly:** The best method I have found was first described by wilderness survival expert Peter Kummerfeldt. I use this lean-to method most of the time, and it works really well for building a fire on deep snow or ice:

- Lay down a layer of green wood on the ground. Lay another layer of green wood across the bottom layer.

This is how to stage a lean-to style fire. (From left) Ignition source, tinder, fatwood, firestarter, small sticks, larger wood, chunks of wood. Once one batch of wood is lit, stack the next bundle crossways. Ignition should be fast and effective.

- Lay a larger log horizontally to the direction the wind is blowing.
- Get the tinder bundle going and prepare to stack the wood.
- On the lee side of the log, where the wind isn't blowing as hard, place the lighted tinder bundle on the green wood.
- Quickly add the intermediate wood by propping it between the log and the green wood.
- Add the larger wood to the fire by crossing it over the intermediate wood.

There are other stacking methods and patterns, including the tipi style and log cabin. The tipi is just like you'd imagine: Lean the sticks into each other, so the pile resembles a tipi. Log cabin style means the wood is stacked in a square around the ignited tinder bundle, like a log cabin.

Practice, and choose the stacking style that you like best.

10. **Gather wood immediately:** If you're going to have enough wood to last through the night, get busy. If there are other people who need something to do, have them begin hauling in all the wood they can find. If dusk is approaching, you'll have limited time to search before it gets completely dark.

How much firewood is enough? Gather an inordinately large pile, then double it. If you'll be depending on the fire for warmth, you can't have too much firewood.

Finally, think about the fire you need to start immediately, and then think about the next one. If you will need tinder, gather that now. If you may need charcloth, make a batch with this fire so you won't run out in the future.

If you are out of ignition materials, figure out how a coal can be preserved or carried to the next campsite. Look around for a tin can, moss, ashes, etc. to insulate and keep the coal smoldering.

Your campfire can be a lifesaver—make sure you can start it and keep it going.

The ability to quickly build a campfire can save your life.

Remember This:

Fire can be a life saver. Used responsibly, it is a cheerful servant that, among other things, helps stave off hypothermia, provides light, cooks food, and boils water. But fire can also be a roaring, blazing hellion that torches and destroys everything in its path.

Before doing anything about starting a fire, make sure it can be controlled. Then, make sure you have several *different* methods of ignition, and efficient fire starter. Know where to find dry kindling and wood, and the best way to stack wood for a campfire.

Practice these skills. Then, should you ever need a fire to survive, building one, regardless of the circumstances, will not be a big deal.

CONCLUSION
WHY PREPARING IS IMPORTANT

Preparedness is a journey and an ongoing project that will help you survive almost any emergency or disaster. Learn the basics of bushcraft and wilderness survival so you can add or subtract equipment, techniques, and philosophies as needed for the situation. Of all things you might gain from this book, the most important is learning to create your own survival mindset. Your most important survival tool—to quote the old, mossy cliché—is between your ears. Use the steps listed in Chapter 1 and S.T.O.P. With the important skill of a survival mindset, you'll be way ahead of everyone else around you.

Thanks for reading! Stay prepared, stay safe.

Leon Pantenburg on the Mississippi River with Quapaw Canoe Company, Spring 2018.